Dining Down Memory Lane

A Collection of Classic Baltimore Restaurants and their Recipes

Shelley Howell

ISBN: 978-0-692-16245-3

Library of Congress Control Number: 2018910113

Illustrations: Heather McCarthy

Creative Direction and Cover/Interior Design: FatCat Studios

Cover Mural "Highlandtown Shakedown" by Ezra Berger

Photographs and Images: Shelley Howell

Editor: Bear Press Editorial Services

Project Editors: Donna Shear and Mike Barth

Printed in the United States of America

Published by: Baltimore Memory Lane Publishing

Towson, Maryland 21204

This book is dedicated to Mac—my soul mate,
my best friend and my perfect partner in life.

Contents

PART TWO: BALTIMORE COUNTY

Foreword

As a lifelong Baltimorean, I have taken great joy in reading this beautiful book. *Dining Down Memory Lane*, not only is it a lovely read, it evokes a nostalgia for the restaurants and their signature dishes. What struck me is the beauty of the illustrations and the wave of memories that I felt as I leafed through the pages. It made me want to go back in time and dine at those famous Baltimore cafes, bakeries, restaurants and tearooms of yesteryear. It used to be that dining was a grand adventure. One that wasn't taken lightly. It called for planning the right outfit and looking ahead to the restaurant's signature dish. Wow, how times have changed!

All of us can pinpoint a time in our lives when we felt sheer joy around a dining experience. I guarantee you will read this book and summon forward one of those tantalizing moments. The book references Elizabeth Large, the *Baltimore Sun* restaurant critic, who writes about the ho-hum experience of dining in today's world and challenges her readers to make a list of restaurants from the past that they remember fondly. Make your own list of "Top Ten Restaurants That You Miss Terribly" and you will find not only those restaurants mentioned here, but your favorite dish and its recipe referenced as well.

I have so many wonderful memories of these once thriving local landmark restaurants. I will always remember my mother taking me to Hutzler's Department Store as a young child and having to get the shrimp salad on cheese bread every time. Delicious! Or the crab cakes at Angelina's that my college boyfriend and I enjoyed so much. Or the many times I took clients to Harvey's Restaurant at Green Spring Station as a young professional where the Boursin cheese spread was complimentary. So many memories and all of the most beloved recipes are chronicled here. What a treasure!

The book is divided by neighborhoods and references the best restaurants in those areas as well as details the most sought after dishes on the menu. Every recipe is a gem and memories come flooding back to me as I turn each page because either I dined at the establishment or remember the lore around the dining experience. The recollections are great but having the recipes available is the "icing on the cake!!" You may not have been to any of these restaurants, but I guarantee you will enjoy the look back and want to make one or more of the recipes.

The author and my friend Shelley, has been thinking about this book for a long time and I never knew it. A lover of a good meal, Shelley had been nostalgic for those beloved restaurants of Baltimore's past and thought this book would strike a chord with so many Baltimoreans as it did with her. She did her research and has assembled a treasure trove of favorite dishes at some of the best restaurants of Baltimore's past.

Shelley and I met volunteering for the MDSPCA. Both of us have been long time supporters and Shelley sat on committees for six years with me when I chaired the March for the Animals. In addition, she has fostered innumerable animals and takes on the tasks no one else wants to do such as staying up all night bottle feeding newborn orphaned kittens. I have always thought of Shelley as a lovely person with exceptional taste and now she has brought us this exceptional book. She brings the same depth of character and love of important things to this ode to Baltimore restaurants.

I hope you enjoy this book as much as I do and it brings a smile to your face as you remember those favorite meals of years past. I can't wait to make the strawberry pie from Haussner's! This book will definitely be a "go to" gift for me. I plan on giving it for holidays, birthdays, bridal showers, and more.

Enjoy the trip down memory lane and bon appétit!

Barb Clapp, CEO Clapp Communications, Baltimore, MD 21209

Preface

Stepping Back in Time

"It seems what we should do is take all the restaurants we have
that sell seared ahi tuna, crab quesadillas, and buffalo anything
and cut their numbers in half. Next, we bring back all the restaurants
that offered terrapin soup, lobster thermidor, chateaubriand
and tableside cherries jubilee."

—Posted by Robert from Cross Keys, 2008

Robert was responding to Baltimore Sun restaurant critic Elizabeth Large's blog, Dining @ Large. A week earlier Elizabeth had encouraged her readers to consider her next installment which would be on the topic of the *Top Ten Restaurants We Miss Terribly*. She knew everyone's list would be different, but Robert's comment resonated with me. He got it too; I was not alone.

Perhaps it's my middle age, but for some time now I have been reminiscing about days gone by. I feel fortunate to have grown up in Lutherville during the 1960s and 1970s. My small close-knit family comprised my parents, my two little sisters, and my paternal grandparents who lived nearby. One way my grandparents forged a connection with us was to take us out for many Saturday night dinners. I always anticipated these nights because *they* were occasions, and we treated them as such. Dresses, party shoes and Shirley Temples anyone?

My earliest fine dining memory would have to be dinner at The Chesapeake. There I was, about 7 or 8, seated at a candle-lit table in the clubby dining room with live piano music playing in the background. I feel certain this was a Saturday night because the dining room hummed with a special energy and every table was full. I ordered my first Crab Imperial, kicking off a lifetime love affair with the stuff! Following dinner, the grown-ups sipped their after-dinner drinks while my sister Rebecca and I found heaven in our coconut snowball desserts. Yum!

I've always collected cookbooks, but several years ago I began a more focused search for Baltimore restaurant recipes, more specifically, recipes from my favorite landmark restaurants that were no longer in business. I was hoping to come across a local cookbook that covered this subject but soon realized that it didn't exist -- thus, the idea for this book. The reader response to the *Top Ten Restaurants We Miss Most* really warmed my heart, confirming my notion that nostalgia is more than just remembering; it's an emotion evoked by memories of things we loved. Here are a few of the comment threads:

Mary in York posted: "Haussner's without a doubt; loved the strawberry pie and basket of assorted muffins and rolls. I was lucky to make a trip back to Maryland with my hubby just before the restaurant closed so he could experience it. I grew up nearby many years ago and remember when there would be a line waiting to get in.

"I had many a chicken salad and tomato aspic at the Women's Exchange...and remember being scolded if I didn't finish my lunch."

Ruth Bogg posted: "The Chesapeake on Charles Street - their Oysters Chesapeake was to die for!"

Elizabeth Large posted: "Louie's the Bookstore and Café in Mount Vernon. I miss that Chestertown Chicken. Why didn't I get that recipe?"

Bill Me posted: "I miss that Chestertown Chicken too. Any chance one of your readers was an old employee with the recipe to share?"

And I really love this one from The Old Line's *Baltimore Gone but Not Forgotten Restaurants*:

"I miss Angelina's on Harford Rd just inside the city limits. It used to be around the corner from the house that I grew up in. They had the best crab cakes in the city. I remember one Christmas eve after coming home from Mass, it was snowing so hard that we couldn't drive anywhere. My mom and I walked to Angelina's in the snow and had crab cakes and it was the best Christmas eve that I can remember." It was posted by Alexander Gnardellis.

My research only reconfirmed the sentiment that we Baltimoreans hold so dear. Over the years many have written in to the Baltimore Sun's *Recipe Finder* in search of this or that lost restaurant recipe, so they could recreate it at home. A quick internet search will produce a random recipe or two, but what I wanted was a whole cookbook of these gems. I didn't find one, so I set myself to the task of writing the book I was looking for: the one-stop place on our bookshelves that Baltimore's memorable restaurants so richly deserve.

Baltimore's early cuisine was largely defined by our proximity to the Chesapeake Bay, *and* a preponderance of German immigrants in the late 19th and early 20th centuries. Fine dining rooms were typically located in the city's grand hotels where waiters served Maryland diamondback terrapin and canvasback duck, Maryland oysters, Eastern Shore chicken and Chesapeake Bay crabs. *Dining Down Memory Lane* covers an era when Continental cuisine and Maryland seafood were predominant.

Cooking and creating dishes are things I really enjoy, but I am not a classically trained chef. I am simply a home cook like many of you. While I have successfully reproduced many of the recipes in this book; they have not been professionally tested. I have made every attempt possible to maintain the integrity of the original recipes as I found them.

One might be tempted to say: "I can't believe we really ate like that," but that's just it - you can't judge by today's standards because our tastes *have* evolved, perhaps becoming more sophisticated. We're certainly far more health conscious and more aware of ethnic cuisines. The '90s would become known for a new generation of restaurants serving up New American or nouvelle cuisine. This resulted in the demise of many restaurants that didn't follow suit.

So many wonderful restaurants have closed over the years, but the ones that I chose for this book hold some personal significance for me. More than just the meals themselves, each of these establishments offered distinct qualities that contributed to my experiences. I have included a wide selection of restaurants, and their recipes, in hopes of sparking a fun dialogue about past, present, and the way we relate to our local cuisine. These restaurants represent a part of who we are as Baltimoreans. So, with that said, maybe it's time to have that retro dinner party you've been thinking about. Who says you can't go home?

Acknowledgements

I must start by thanking each one of you for purchasing a copy of this book. For me, this has been an absolute labor of love and I have tried my best to offer a book that you will be proud to own. Finding these recipes and sharing them with you brings an instant feeling of sentimental joy. This book has quite literally been years in the making, so it is impossible for me to thank everyone who has inspired me along the way and I cannot overstate what a group effort this has been.

To my gifted editor at Bear Press Editorial Services: my heartfelt thanks, not only for polishing my manuscript, but for your coaching and guidance; you made my book into a reality.

My sincere thanks and appreciation to Donna Shear and Mike Barth; for your editing contributions.

I tip my hat with gratitude to everyone on the FatCat Studios team for all my design elements including the greatest cover design I could ever imagine. Heather McCarthy - your skill at illustration is amazing and I feel so honored to have your beautiful pen-and-ink sketches in this book. And to Erin Snider - thank you for your detailed attention with regards to creative illustration and layout production. Special thanks to "Top Cat" Valentia McVey - foremost for your genuine enthusiasm and belief in this book. I knew from our first phone call that I needn't look any further. BOOM!

I was absolutely elated that Barb Clapp agreed to do the foreword for this book! She is the CEO of Clapp Communications, an award-winning communications agency specializing in public relations, media buying and marketing here in Baltimore. To Barb: My deepest and heartfelt thanks. You are an absolute dynamo and truly inspire me to be a better person. I am so grateful that you are a part of this book and feel fortunate to call you my friend.

To the gifted leaders and individuals who participated in this project: Marshall Adams, Anna Aladiev, Ezra Berger, David Brown, Jim Considine, Aliceann Howell, E. Scott Johnson, Esq., Patricia McKay, Diane Mitchell, Meg Schwartzman Schudel, and Leslie Udoff; *Thank you* - my sincere appreciation for your time and interest, encouragement and ongoing support.

A shout out to James H. "Mackie" McKay III, my partner in crime, for your steadfast determination and unwavering belief in me; you made me realize my dreams.

A special thank-you to my family - my mother (Ann) and my sisters (Rebecca and Emily); for your unconditional love, humor and good cheer. Only one regret - that my late father, H. Thomas Howell, is not here to see this book.

Lastly, I owe a debt of gratitude to the restaurateurs of Baltimore, whose establishments provided me with such enduring memories and inspiration, without whom this book simply would not have been possible.

XO Shelley

PART I: BALTIMORE CITY

Otterbein

Hampton's
at the Harbor Court Hotel
550 Light Street

1986 – 2006

*C*ondé Nast Traveler named Hampton's as one of the top two restaurants in America and it certainly was the epitome of fine dining and elegance. Featuring innovative seasonal American cuisine with an award-winning wine list and exquisite service, Hampton's was considered the finest restaurant of its time in Baltimore.

The dining room was grandly elegant, dressed in salmon-colored silk moiré, fine art, antique mahogany breakfronts, and Villeroy & Boch china. Tables were adorned with bowls of floating magnolias, and guests relaxed in comfortable, oversized armchairs while dining at a leisurely pace, taking in the breathtaking view of the night-lit harbor. Open only for dinner and Sunday brunch, the dress was formal, requiring men to wear jackets and ties.

Entrées were artfully arranged under silver-domed lids and presented by tuxedoed waiters who lifted the domes in dramatic unison. Sorbets were served between courses, and it wasn't unusual for the dining experience to last three hours. Executive Chef, Michael Rork, who opened Hampton's, said his bosses supplied him with any ingredient he requested. He added: "It was perfect, like a playground."

Mango Gazpacho

If you are a fan of classic gazpacho soup, then try this refreshing take. On a hot summer day this fruity, tropical version is a winner. Make the gazpacho a day in advance if you like but prepare the tian just before serving.

Serves: 4

+ **2** large mangoes, peeled and sliced from the pit
+ **2 tablespoons** freshly squeezed lime juice
+ **¼ cup** extra virgin olive oil
+ **½** roasted yellow pepper
+ **¼ cup** red onion, chopped
+ **1** large cucumber, peeled, seeded and chopped
+ **½ teaspoon** ancho chili, (more to taste)

+ **¼ cup** scallions, chopped
+ **2** stalks celery, chopped
+ **¼ cup** orange juice, freshly squeezed

Tian:
+ **1 cup** lump crab meat, picked clean
+ **4** small avocados, diced
+ **2** small tomatoes, peeled, seeded and diced

Garnish:
+ **½ cup** cilantro, chopped

In blender or food processor, combine mango, lime juice, olive oil, yellow bell pepper, red onion, cucumber, ancho chili, scallions, celery, and orange juice. Puree. Cover and set aside.

Divide the tian equally between 4 large soup bowls by layering avocado, tomato, crab and more avocado in the center of each bowl.

Ladle gazpacho in equal portions around layered tian. Garnish with a sprinkle of cilantro.

Adapted from: Deseret News, by Diane Howard, May 25, 1999

Swiss Chard and Spinach Turnovers

Switzerland was celebrating its 700th anniversary in 1991, and executive chef, Michael Rork, offered a Swiss selection on the menu every evening that summer. These wonderful little turnovers make an impressive presentation and flavorful starter. To save time, the vegetable mixture can be made a day ahead and refrigerated.

Serves: 4 to 6

Vegetable Mixture:
+ **16 ounces** Swiss chard leaves, stems removed
+ **8 ounces** fresh spinach
+ **1** large onion, finely chopped
+ **2 ounces** butter
+ **1 cup** heavy cream
+ **2 tablespoons** pinenuts

Preheat oven to 400°.

+ **4 ounces** raisins
+ **6 tablespoons** Gruyere cheese, grated
+ Salt and freshly ground pepper to taste
+ **1** sheet puff pastry
+ **1** egg white
+ **1** egg yolk
+ Sauce (recipe follows)

Wash Swiss chard and separate leaves from shoots. Coarsely chop Swiss chard and spinach. Heat butter in a large skillet and sauté onion until translucent. Add chard and spinach. Sauté briefly to wilt. Stir in cream and bring to a boil. Lower heat and add pinenuts, raisins and cheese. Cook about 10 minutes, or until thickened. Season with salt and pepper. Allow this vegetable mixture to cool.

Roll out puff pastry to a thickness of 1/16". Cut out circles with 3" diameters. Place two tablespoons vegetable mixture in center. Brush the edges with egg white. Fold into semicircles pressing the edges together. Place turnovers on a buttered baking sheet or line with parchment. Brush with egg yolk. Bake for 5 to 7 minutes, or until golden brown.

Sauce:
+ **1** onion, finely chopped
+ **1-ounce** butter
+ **1 cup** heavy cream
+ **2 tablespoons** Gruyere cheese, grated

+ **1 tablespoon** chervil, finely chopped
+ **1** tomato, skinned, seeded, juiced and diced
+ Fresh herbs for garnishing.

Heat butter in a small saucepan and sauté onion. Stir in cream. Add cheese, chervil, and tomatoes. Stir well. Boil until sauce reaches creamy consistency. Season with salt and pepper.

Coat plates with sauce. Set turnovers in center and garnish with fresh herbs.

Adapted from: The Baltimore Sun, by Heather Locke, July 31, 1991

Grilled Leg of Lamb with Anchor Steam Sauce

This hearty entrée was specially prepared for a group of gourmands and was such a success it made its way to the menu. Executive chef, Holly Forbes said she wanted to bring an element of playfulness to Hampton's.

Serves: 6

+ **1 5-pound** leg of lamb, deboned, butterflied and pounded lightly
+ 1 head of garlic, roasted in 400° oven for approximately 40 minutes (see note)
+ **½ cup** of fresh herbs, chopped (basil, rosemary, sage, or other combination to taste)
+ Kosher salt, to taste
+ Freshly ground pepper, to taste
+ **½ cup** olive oil, approximately
+ Anchor Steam Sauce (recipe follows)

Preheat oven to 325°.

Rub one side of leg of lamb with salt and pepper. Drizzle with half of olive oil and rub that in. Squeeze out the roasted garlic and rub that in. Sprinkle with chopped herbs. Roll up jelly-roll fashion and tie with butcher's twine. Rub outside with remaining olive oil, salt, and pepper to taste. Sear in roasting pan over medium heat until browned on all sides. Finish in oven, cooking approximately 15 minutes per pound. Or grill for about 2 ½ hours, until preferred degree of doneness is reached. Serve with Anchor Steam Sauce.

Anchor Steam Sauce:
Makes: about 4 cups

+ **2 bottles** Anchor Steam beer
+ **2 bottles** Beck's dark beer
+ 1 head of garlic, cloves peeled
+ 1 large onion, chopped
+ **1 can** beef broth
+ **1 can** chicken broth
+ **2** carrots, chopped
+ **1** bay leaf
+ Several sprigs of thyme
+ Salt and pepper to taste
+ **2 to 3 tablespoons** cornstarch mixed with **2 tablespoons** of water

Put all ingredients in nonreactive pan and cook over medium-high heat until liquid is reduced by half. Strain and return to pan. Add salt and pepper to taste, thicken lightly, with cornstarch (use only what you need to reach desired consistency), adjust seasoning.

Note: Roast the garlic first. For best results, cut off top quarter of bulb and rub in a bit of olive oil, wrap tightly in aluminum foil. Place on a cookie sheet. Do not let the garlic burn.

Adapted from: The Baltimore Sun, by Karol V. Menzie, September 14, 1994

Rockfish in a Potato Crust with a Plum Tomato Compote and Brown Butter-Balsamic Vinaigrette

Rockfish (striped bass) is the official fish of the State of Maryland and with good reason. Its mild, sweet flavor and prevalence in the waters of the Chesapeake Bay make it a local favorite.

Serves: 6

+ **3** large baking potatoes, peeled and grated

+ **3** egg whites

+ **1 tablespoon** parsley, finely chopped

+ **1 tablespoon** chives, finely chopped

+ Salt and white pepper to taste

+ **6** rockfish fillets, skin on **(6 ounces each)**

Plum-tomato compote:
+ **6** shallots, peeled

+ **3 tablespoons** olive oil

+ **9** medium plum tomatoes, quartered

+ **1 teaspoon** garlic, minced

+ **12** leaves fresh basil, julienne

+ **2 tablespoons** balsamic vinegar

Vinaigrette:
+ **1-pound** butter

+ **2 tablespoons** balsamic vinegar

Preheat oven to 350°.

In a large mixing bowl, combine the grated potatoes with the egg whites, parsley, chives, salt, and white pepper. Cover the flesh side of fillets completely with the potato mixture.

In a large sauté pan, heat olive oil until very hot. Carefully sear the fish, potato side down, until golden brown. Turn fillets over and finish cooking.

Plum-tomato compote: Sauté the shallots in 1 tablespoon olive oil. Wrap in aluminum foil. Place in oven and roast until soft.

In a saucepan place 2 tablespoons olive oil, tomatoes, roasted shallots and garlic. Cook until heated through. Add the basil and balsamic vinegar. Season with salt and white pepper.

Vinaigrette: In a saucepan, over medium heat, melt the butter and cook to a golden-brown color. Remove from heat. Cool slightly and add the balsamic vinegar.

To serve, drizzle serving plates with the vinaigrette, then top with the fillet and compote.

Adapted from: Cooking Secrets by Kathleen DeVanna Fish

Champagne Truffle Risotto

This recipe from executive chef, Michael Rork, can easily be served as an entrée with the addition of some pancetta or prosciutto. Risotto is a labor of love and requires both time and attention, but the result is so worth it!

Serves: 8 to 10 as a side dish

+ **1 pound** short-grained Arborio rice
+ **½ cup** olive oil
+ **2 cups** chicken stock
+ **1 cup** champagne

+ **3 ounces** truffle peelings
+ **½ cup** whipping cream
+ **1 cup** parmesan cheese

In a large heavy saucepan, combine rice and olive oil; stir over medium heat.

Slowly add chicken stock, a little at a time, until all is fully absorbed before adding more stock. Risotto should be tender and sticky, but not fully cooked.

Add champagne and truffles and reduce by half.

Just before serving, add cream and cheese and reduce slowly, stirring occasionally, until rice is tender.

Adapted from: The Milwaukee Sentinel, June 2, 1994

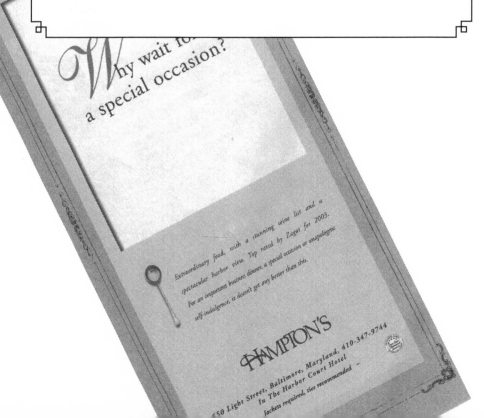

Why wait for a special occasion?

Extraordinary food, with a stunning wine list and a spectacular harbor view. Top rated by Zagat for 2003. For an important business dinner, a special occasion or unapologetic self-indulgence, it doesn't get any better than this.

HAMPTON'S
In The Harbor Court Hotel
550 Light Street, Baltimore, Maryland, 410-347-9744
Jackets required, ties recommended

Apple and Almond Tart with Melted Brie

This delicious dessert takes on a European flair with its pairing of apples and cheese.

Serves: 6

Dough:
+ **1 ½ cups** butter, melted
+ **½ cup** sugar
+ **1** egg
+ **2 ¼ cups** flour
+ Pinch of salt

Filling:
+ **½ cup** plus **4 tablespoons** butter, melted
+ **¾ cup** sugar
+ **1 cup** almonds, toasted and ground
+ **4** large eggs
+ **6 tablespoons** flour
+ **4** Granny Smith apples
+ Cinnamon sugar
+ **8 ounces** brie cheese

Preheat oven to 350°.

Dough: Blend melted butter and sugar together until mixture becomes light and fluffy. Add the egg to the mixture and stir until well combined. Mix in the flour and salt, stirring well. Roll out dough on a floured surface and line individual greased tart pans.

Filling: In a large bowl, combine ½ cup melted butter, sugar, and almonds together and mix until it becomes light and fluffy. Add the eggs and blend until fully incorporated. Add the flour, mixing well.

Fill each tart shell almost to the top with the filling. Slice Granny Smith apples and arrange slices on top of the filling. Brush with 4 tablespoons melted butter and sprinkle with cinnamon sugar.

Bake until well browned. When just cool enough to handle, unmold and top with a wedge of brie cheese.

Place back in a warm oven to melt the brie slightly. Serve immediately.

Adapted from: Cooking Secrets by Kathleen DeVanna Fish

Fell's Point

Obrycki's
1727 East Pratt Street

1944 - 2011

The mother of all Baltimore food traditions - The Crab Feast. "Everybody has their favorite crab house," said Marty Katz, the Maryland editor for Zagat guide. "But for out-of-towners, Obrycki's became the face of steamed crabs in Baltimore, and it was still as original a crab-house experience as a visitor could hope to get." It didn't hurt when in 1981 the influential New York Times food critic, Craig Claiborne wrote, "A week or so ago I shared an experience that turned out to be one of the headiest, most exhilarating and gratifying days of my life. It included...the finest crabmeat feast I have [ever] been witness to or participated in." Claiborne's review of Obrycki's went on to refer to it as "one of my favorite dining spots on earth." His column changed the playing field.

Owners Rose and Richard Cernak purchased Obrycki's from its original owner, Ed Obrycki in 1976. Originally known as Ed Obrycki's Olde Crab House, the restaurant was located inside two rowhouses at East Pratt and Regester Streets. Around 1986, the Cernaks purchased a warehouse across the street allowing for larger dining rooms, more than doubling their seating capacity. Because crabs are seasonal, the restaurant was only open from April to November.

Obrycki's was never about fine dining; it was for crab picking which meant tables covered with brown paper, guests outfitted in lobster bibs, lots of paper napkins, crab mallets, and beer by the pitcher. The dining rooms were quite spacious, utilizing lots of exposed brick archways and warm colors. The aroma of vinegar and spices was immediately welcoming, stirring the senses, while the wait staff was happy to instruct the novice tourist on the art of conquering the steamed blue crab. One of the traits that made Obrycki's unique from other crab houses was their use of a secret black pepper seasoning, which enhanced the sweet crabmeat, and the absence of the more traditional Old Bay. Besides hard-shell crabs, the menu offered a variety of other seafood items, but the real draw was the steamed crabs.

My family, who happened to be friends of Rose and Richard, spent many a birthday celebration at Obrycki's with the Cernaks and other friends. We would be seated in the rear dining room at a very long table with dozens upon dozens of steamed crabs piled up before us. Our guests looked forward to good times at the restaurant, and I don't recall anyone ever taking a pass! Everyone wanted to visit the crab house including celebrities like Danny DeVito, Neil Diamond, Bette Midler, Daniel Craig, Nicole Kidman, and U2's Bono. It was even listed in the book *1000 Places to See Before You Die*.

Today the Cernaks' offspring operate two Obrycki's locations at BWI-Thurgood Marshall Airport. While steamed crabs are not on the menu, guests can indulge in crab cakes, the house specialty, and they also have a thriving online internet business at Obryckis.com where customers can order steamed crabs and the secret black pepper seasoning.

Chesapeake Bay Crabs

This tried-and-true Baltimore classic came from Obrycki's owner Rob Cernak. It's essential to keep the crabs on ice before steaming.

Serves: 6

+ **1 tablespoon** white vinegar
+ **1 eight-ounce** bottle of beer
+ **36** crabs
+ Crab seasoning

Add 6 cups of water, the vinegar, and the beer to an 8-gallon stockpot fitted with a raised rack. Alternately, if you don't have a raised rack, use clean, cloth wrapped bricks to raise the rack about 6" from the bottom. It is important that the crabs are not submerged while they are being steamed.

Make a layer of crabs on the rack and cover them with crab seasoning to taste, anywhere from ⅛" to ¾" of seasoning. Repeat in layers. Bring the liquid to a boil. When the steam begins to rise above the crabs, cover the pot with the lid and allow to steam for 30 to 40 minutes, or until the crabs are bright red. Remove the crabs with tongs or rubber gloves.

Adapted from: www.marthastewart.com

Obrycki's Coleslaw

Rose's coleslaw can be prepared a day before serving allowing for the flavors to marry.

Serves: 8

+ **1 ½ pounds** cabbage, finely shredded
+ **½ teaspoon** salt
+ **1 ¼ cups** mayonnaise
+ **¼ cup** white vinegar
+ **¼ cup** sugar
+ **½ tablespoon** onion, minced
+ **¼ cup** grated carrots

Mix together all ingredients except cabbage. When mixed well, add the cabbage. Chill before serving.

Adapted from: The Baltimore Sun, July 28, 1999

Baked Stuffed Shrimp

This is one of those great "do it ahead of company coming" dishes that you can prepare early in the day up to the baking point.

Serves: 4 as an entrée or 8 as an appetizer

+ **16** jumbo shrimp, peeled, deveined, leaving tails intact
+ **1-pound** backfin crab meat
+ **⅔ cup** fresh breadcrumbs, seasoned with **¼ teaspoon** seafood seasoning
+ **1** egg, beaten
+ Mayonnaise
+ Paprika

Preheat oven to 350°.

Lightly spray an oblong glass baking dish with cooking spray. Carefully mix seasoned crumbs and crab meat, then add beaten egg and gently mix again.

Divide crab mixture into 16 portions. Top each shrimp with the mixture, covering the shrimp completely but leaving tails exposed. With a spatula, spread the mayonnaise lightly over the topping and sprinkle with paprika. Bake 20 minutes, or until shrimp are cooked and the tops are golden brown.

Adapted from: The Baltimore Sun, July 13, 1974

Maryland Crab Cakes

With minimal filler, these pan-fried crab cakes allow the crab to remain the true star.

Serves: 4

+ 6 saltine crackers
+ **1-pound** jumbo lump crabmeat, picked over
+ 1 large egg
+ **2 tablespoons** mayonnaise
+ **1 teaspoon** freshly squeezed lemon juice

+ **1 teaspoon** Worcestershire sauce
+ Coarse salt and freshly ground pepper, to taste
+ **3 tablespoons** vegetable oil

In a large bowl, carefully mix together first seven ingredients. The mixture should be wet. Divide the mixture into four equal portions and shape into crab cakes.

Heat the vegetable oil over medium heat in a large nonstick skillet. Gently slide the crab cakes off a spatula into the hot oil. Cook the crab cakes until golden brown; about 4-5 minutes per side. Remove from the skillet and drain on paper towels. Serve warm.

Adapted from: www.epicurious.com, April 7, 2010

My family celebrates a birthday with a crab feast at Obrycki's. In the foreground are owners Rose and Richard Cernak.

Eclairs Supreme

Most eclairs are filled with a custard cream. Obrycki's "famous" eclairs call for ice cream and I recommend serving them with a top-notch French vanilla.

Serves: 10 to 12

+ Puff Pastry (recipe follows)
+ Vanilla ice cream
+ Chocolate Sauce (recipe follows)
+ English walnut pieces
+ Shredded coconut
+ Maraschino cherries

Puff Pastry for Eclairs:
+ **1 cup** water

+ **3 ounces** butter, cut into pieces
+ **1 teaspoon** salt
+ **1/8 teaspoon** vanilla
+ **1 teaspoon** sugar
+ Pinch of nutmeg
+ **1 cup** sifted all-purpose flour
+ 4 large eggs

Preheat oven to 425°.

Bring water to boil in a saucepan. Add butter, salt, vanilla, sugar and nutmeg, stirring to melt butter. Remove pan from heat and add flour all at once. Beat the flour until completely blended. Over medium heat, beat vigorously with a wooden spoon until mixture separates from the sides of pan and forms a mass in the middle of pot.

Remove pan from heat and make an indentation in the middle of the mass. Break one egg into the center of the well and beat until absorbed. Repeat the procedure with two more eggs. When the mixture is smooth, fill a pastry bag fitted with a large plain tip to pipe pastry onto greased cookie sheets. Space oblong mounds 2" apart, and brush with an egg wash mixture; ½ teaspoon water and 1 beaten egg.

Bake in oven for 20 minutes. Reduce heat to 375° and bake an additional 10 minutes. Remove from oven, making 1" slits in sides, and return to oven (leaving door ajar) for 10 minutes. Remove from oven, slit eclairs in half, and remove the damp centers. Allow to cool or freeze. When ready to serve, fill with vanilla ice cream, and drizzle with Chocolate Sauce. Sprinkle with shredded coconut and walnuts, and top with a cherry before serving.

Chocolate Sauce:
+ **9 ounces** good quality semi-sweet chocolate
+ **2 ½ tablespoons** unsalted butter

+ **1 cup** milk
+ **3 tablespoons** heavy cream
+ **¼ cup** sugar

Melt chocolate and butter in the top of double boiler over hot water. Beat until smooth.

In a separate saucepan, bring milk and cream to a boil with the sugar, stirring to dissolve. Whisk mixture into melted chocolate. Can be served hot or at room temperature.

Adapted from: Dining In - Baltimore, Vol. II by Mary Lou Baker and Bonnie Rapoport Marshall

Highlandtown

Haussner's
3244 Eastern Avenue

1926-1999

Few would argue that the legendary Haussner's could be considered one of Baltimore's most famous landmark restaurants, if not *the* most famous. William Henry Haussner emigrated from Bavaria and founded the small restaurant at 3313 Eastern Avenue in 1926. Ten years later he would buy five rowhouses down the block and convert them into what would become a huge restaurant seating 500 people. He met and married his future wife, Frances Wilke Haussner, a fellow German immigrant, after a three-week courtship in 1935. It turned out that 19th-century European and American art was the couple's shared passion.

Frances bought her first painting to mark their fourth anniversary in 1939: *The Venetian Flower Vendor* by Eugene de Blaas. They hung the painting over the pastry counter. Haussner's became home to a vast collection of original European paintings acquired through both auctions and private collectors. These would eventually cover almost every inch of the restaurant's walls. They never paid more than $3000 for any one piece. Additionally, there were bronzes, marble busts, and wood carvings. The most impressive painting, in terms of size, was the 18,000 square-foot *"Pantheon de la Guerre."* It comprised a series of panels located on the museum-like second floor. The painting commemorates the Allied effort in the first World War, and today can be viewed at the Liberty Memorial in Kansas City.

Haussner's had several large dining rooms where each table was set with white linen tablecloths and napkins. Between the lighting and the paintings, Haussner's offered an "Old World" quality. The kitchen served traditional German cuisine and American comfort food. William, a master chef, had been trained in some of Europe's best hotel kitchens. Haussner's was closed on Sunday, Monday and Christmas. They didn't accept reservations, so on nights they were open a long line of locals and tourists was always wrapped around the building. The seasoned waitresses wore white uniforms and white shoes and often helped patrons navigate the unbelievably extensive menu. It wasn't unusual for the staff to serve 1600 meals on a Saturday, with a menu that included ninety entrees and thirty vegetables.

As for desserts, the most popular was Haussner's strawberry pie prepared by their own in-house bakery. William passed away in 1963 but the restaurant would survive for thirty-six years beyond that. Frances employed a full-time staff of 220. In later years the restaurant was operated by the Haussners' daughter, Frances George and her husband, Steve.

I will never forget the first time I went there. It was 1987 and I had recently gotten engaged. I had already purchased my wedding gown, but I still had to find the perfect wedding shoes. I asked my mother if she would like to go with me down to Highlandtown where many a bride went in those days. I wanted to get a second opinion, her opinion. I happened to find those shoes at a little shop right on Eastern Avenue. As we walked out my mother said, "Let's go to Haussner's for lunch and celebrate!" Of course, I was familiar with the famous Haussner's, but I had never gotten around to going there. We all know how that story goes. It was quite an experience! A visual overload, but in a good way. Between the endless framed master paintings, the lengthy menu, and just having my mother to myself, it was time well spent.

On Wednesday, October 6, 1999, Haussner's served its last meal. Less than a month later, on November 2, Sotheby's Auction House in New York sold the most valuable paintings in the collection for more than $10 million (Rod Stewart bought one). Included were pieces from the estates of J.P. Morgan, Cornelius Vanderbilt and Henry Walters. The other 80% of the collection was later auctioned off locally at the Richard Opfer Auctioneering House in Timonium. The first item to go was the gigantic ball of string. The ball had been started during the '70s from the string that bound the rented napkin bundles. It measured 337.5 miles and weighed 825 pounds! Frances had come up with the idea to remind staff how expensive the napkins were. She didn't want them to be used for cleaning. So, every time a new bundle was unwrapped, the string would be added to the ball. After a bidding war the "Great Ball of String" went for $7500. It now resides at the Antique Man store in Fell's Point. It was even featured in the 2000 film, *Meet the Parents* starring Ben Stiller and Robert De Niro.

More recently, in Season Three of AMC's *Mad Men*, a reproduction of Haussner's was the featured setting in Episode 27 *On the Town*, written by series creator, Matthew Weiner, a Baltimore native. In the episode, characters Don Draper and Salvatore Romano are visiting Baltimore on business and dine at Haussner's, later spending the night at the Belvedere Hotel, and making a trip to Baltimore's London Fog headquarters.

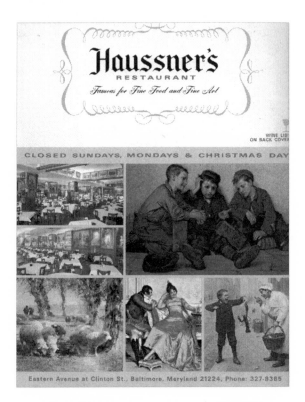

German Potato Salad

This tangy potato salad has the perfect flavor combination of tart and sweet while the addition of bacon just makes everything better. Try this Haussner's dish out at your next picnic or potluck—it's sure to be a conversation starter and crowd-pleaser!

Serves: 4

+ **1-pound** small new potatoes
+ 3 slices bacon
+ 1 medium onion, chopped
+ ½ **cup** white wine vinegar

+ **1 teaspoon** salt
+ Pinch of white pepper
+ **1 tablespoon** sugar

Wash and boil potatoes unpeeled and let cool. Peel and cut into ¼" slices.

Cook bacon in a skillet until crispy, reserving the drippings. Crumble over potatoes.

Using the same skillet, sauté the onions with the reserved drippings until translucent. Add remaining ingredients to pan and bring to a boil. Pour over the potato-bacon mixture and mix well.

Serve warm or at room temperature.

Adapted from: Cooking Secrets by Kathleen DeVanna Fish

Crouton-Filled Potato Dumplings

These are a delicious accompaniment to Haussner's Sauerbraten.

Makes: 12 dumplings

+ **12 1"** sourdough bread cubes
+ **1 ½ pounds** russet potatoes
+ **1 ½ teaspoons** salt
+ **⅛ teaspoon** ground nutmeg
+ **½ cup** (or more) all-purpose flour
+ **½ cup** cornstarch
+ **1** large egg

Preheat oven to 400°.

Evenly space bread cubes on a baking sheet. Bake about 10 minutes or until crisp. Set aside to cool.

Cook whole potatoes in a large pot of salted water, about 45 minutes. Drain and allow to cool. Peel and cut potatoes into large chunks. Refrigerate until chilled, about 30 minutes.

In a large bowl, mash the potatoes. Mix in salt, nutmeg, ½ cup flour, and cornstarch. Knead mixture by hand in bowl until a smooth dough forms. If too sticky, add additional flour. Mix in egg. Using about ¼ cup, form dough into balls and insert a crouton into the center. Roll between palms to completely enclose the crouton. Continue with remaining dumplings.

In a large pot of boiling salted water, cook dumplings in batches for 10 minutes. Drain and transfer dumplings to a large bowl.

Adapted from: Bon Appétit, September 1995

"Highlandtown Shakedown" by muralist Ezra Berger located at 3201 Eastern Avenue.

Creamed Spinach

Maggi is a seasoning sauce that originated in Switzerland. If you can't find it, soy sauce makes a good substitute.

Serves: 8

+ **2 ½ pounds** spinach, thoroughly washed and stems removed
+ **2 quarts** reserved spinach liquid
+ **½ cup** butter
+ **8 tablespoons** flour
+ **2 teaspoons** anchovies
+ Maggi seasoning sauce to taste
+ **⅛ teaspoon** nutmeg
+ Salt and pepper to taste
+ **1** medium onion, chopped
+ **1 cup** light cream

Place the washed spinach in a large pot and cook over low heat for about 5 minutes or until it has wilted. Cool. Drain the spinach and squeeze out all excess moisture reserving the liquid. Chop the spinach finely and set aside.

Sauté the onion gently in oil or butter until golden. Set aside.

Prepare a roux by melting the butter and combining with flour stirring until smooth; cook for a minute over low heat.

Slowly blend the spinach liquid into the roux and add anchovies, Maggi seasoning, nutmeg, salt, and pepper. Allow it to come to a simmer and cook for 3 to 4 minutes. Stir in the spinach and sautéed onions. Stir in cream and heat through before serving.

Adapted from: The Baltimore Sun, January 14, 2014

Sweet-and-Sour Dressing

This recipe doesn't call for oil, but if you prefer a less pungent dressing then add some after the dressing cools down a bit. Use this to dress a fresh garden salad or simply pair it with steamed vegetables.

Yield: 3 cups

+ **2 cups** sugar
+ **2 cups** white vinegar
+ **1 teaspoon** or more to taste, pickling spices tied in cheesecloth

Place all ingredients in a medium saucepan and bring to a boil. Simmer until sugar melts and mixture is translucent again, about 5 minutes. Cool and refrigerate until ready for use.

Adapted from: The Baltimore Sun, October 22, 2003

Sauerbraten

On a chilly winter's night or a Raven's game tailgate, what could be better than this slow-cooked sauerbraten served with dumplings and wilted red cabbage? It requires marinating for several days but is well worth the wait. Try using Otterbein's Ginger Cookies for a true Baltimore-style taste sensation.

Serves: 8

+ 3 ½ **cups** Burgundy
+ **1-quart** vinegar
+ 2 ½ **cups** sugar
+ Juice and rind of **12** lemons
+ **1-pound** onions, chopped
+ **½ cup** mixed pickling spice
+ **2** sticks whole cinnamon

+ **4 pounds** top sirloin butt
+ Flour
+ **1 teaspoon** salt
+ **½ teaspoon** seasoning salt
+ **½ pound** ginger snap cookies, crushed
+ **2** bay leaves

Preheat oven to 350°.

Make a marinade by mixing together 3 cups Burgundy, vinegar, 2 cups sugar, lemons, onions, pickling spice, and cinnamon sticks in a non-reactive container. Completely cover the meat with the marinade and let marinate for a few days in the refrigerator. Remove the meat from the marinade and place it in a roasting pan with about 4 cups of the marinade. Roast the meat for 2 to 3 hours or until done. Remove the meat from the pan. Skim off extra fat from the pan and place it in a saucepan.

Slowly add a little flour to the fat to make a smooth roux. Cook on the stove top so the flour toasts a little. Strain the pan juices and the reserved marinade that was not cooked with the meat into the roux. Add the remaining ½ cup sugar, salt, seasoning salt, ginger snaps, remaining ½ cup Burgundy, and bay leaves whisking together as it comes to a boil. Lower heat and let it simmer about 20 minutes. If too thick, add water; if too thin, reduce a little longer.

Slice meat and place on individual plates. Pour gravy over meat and serve.

Adapted from: Maryland's Historic Restaurants and their recipes by Dawn O'Brien and Rebecca Schenck

Shrimp Charles

A Haussner's original!

Serves: 4

- **24** shrimp in shells, (16/20 count)
- **2 tablespoons** Dijon style mustard
- **1 tablespoon** white wine vinegar
- **1 ½ teaspoons** sugar
- **¼ cup** fresh dill or 1 tablespoon dill weed
- **½ cup** light olive oil

Process mustard, vinegar, sugar, and dill in a food processor or blender. Slowly add in the oil while the processor is running to fully incorporate.

Steam the shrimp about 5 minutes until pink, careful not to overcook. Peel and arrange in a single layer in one dish or individual casseroles. Pour the sauce over the shrimp and broil until bubbly. Serve immediately.

Adapted from: The Baltimore Sun, November 16, 1986

Smithfield Ham and Crab Sauté

Called a sauté but broiled, this dish pairs salty ham which compliments the sweet crab. It can be served as an appetizer or light meal.

Serves: 4

- **1-pound** jumbo lump crabmeat
- **6 ounces** chopped, thinly sliced Smithfield ham
- **½ cup** unsalted butter, melted

Divide crabmeat leaving lumps intact among four individual shallow casseroles. Sprinkle ham over the crab. Drizzle melted butter over the tops and place in a preheated broiler until hot and ham is a little crispy on the edges, about 2 to 4 minutes.

Adapted from: Saveur.com, April 11, 2007

Haussner's Crab Imperial

There are no shortages for crab imperial recipes in Maryland, but Haussner's was somewhat unique in that it used a béchamel sauce.

Serves: 6 as an appetizer

+ **1-pound** lump crabmeat
+ **2** slices white bread
+ **2** eggs, beaten
+ **4 tablespoons** mayonnaise
+ **1 teaspoon** prepared mustard
+ **1 teaspoon** salt

+ **1 teaspoon** black pepper
+ **1 teaspoon** Worcestershire sauce
+ **½ teaspoon** parsley, chopped
+ Béchamel Sauce (recipe follows)
+ **½ teaspoon** paprika

Preheat oven to 350°.

Pick over crabmeat carefully to remove any shells leaving lumps intact. Remove crusts and cut bread into cubes. Combine eggs, mayonnaise, mustard, salt, pepper, and Worcestershire in a medium bowl. Add bread and parsley. Fold in crabmeat carefully by hand to prevent lumps from breaking. Spoon into individual casseroles or dishes. Top each with cream sauce and sprinkle with paprika. Bake for 15 to 20 minutes until golden on top.

Béchamel Sauce:
+ **1 cup** milk
+ **2 tablespoons** butter

+ **2 tablespoons** flour
+ Pinch of salt

Heat milk in a small saucepan. In a separate saucepan, melt butter and combine with flour and salt and cook over medium heat, stirring constantly until mixture is a smooth roux. Add the hot milk in a steady stream, stirring constantly until the sauce is smooth and thick.

Adapted from: Ahistoryofdrinking.com, October 2010

Strawberry Pie

A Baltimore tradition...there was always room left for a slice of Haussner's legendary pie.

Yield: 1 (9-inch) pie

+ 1 ½ **cups** sugar
+ ½ **teaspoon** strawberry flavoring
+ ½ **teaspoon** red food coloring
+ 2 **cups** boiling water
+ 2 **tablespoons** cornstarch dissolved in ½ **cup** water
+ 1 **cup** Pastry Cream (recipe follows)

+ 1 pre-baked deep 9" pie shell
+ 1 ½ **pints** fresh strawberries, washed and hulled (keep whole if small; cut in half lengthwise if large)
+ Whipped cream
+ Toasted, slivered almonds

Glaze: Add the sugar, strawberry flavoring, and food coloring to boiling water. Add dissolved cornstarch to the water/sugar mixture and stir to thicken over medium-high heat. Remove from heat and set aside. Meanwhile, prepare the Pastry Cream and allow it to cool before spreading in the bottom of the pastry shell.

Spread ½ pint of the strawberries evenly over the Pastry Cream covering with half of the sugar/water glaze. Add the remaining strawberries and cover with the remaining glaze. Decorate the edges of the pie with whipped cream and sprinkle with the toasted almonds. Chill and serve.

Pastry Cream:
+ 1 **cup** milk
+ 3 egg yolks
+ ¼ **cup** plus 2 **tablespoons** sugar

+ ¼ **cup** flour
+ 1 ½ **teaspoons** vanilla
+ 1 to 1 ½ **tablespoons** butter, softened

Scald the milk in a large saucepan and set aside. In a medium bowl, whisk together the egg yolks and sugar until light in color and very thick, before beating in the flour. Slowly pour the scalded milk into the egg mixture and blend well. Return the mixture to the saucepan and cook over low heat, stirring constantly with a whisk until the mixture comes to a boil. Keep whisking as the mixture will appear lumpy at first. Be careful not to allow the mixture to stick to the bottom of the pan and burn.

When smooth, remove from heat. Add vanilla and butter. Cover the surface with greased waxed paper to prevent it from forming a skin. Allow it to cool.

Note: The measurements given for the glaze is a lot and makes enough for two pies.

Adapted from: Maryland's Historic Restaurants and Their Recipes by Dawn O'Brien and Rebecca Schenck

Little Italy

Velleggia's
204 South High Street

1937 - 2009

Until it closed Velleggia's was Little Italy's oldest restaurant. What began as a small pub-style eatery evolved into one of the largest establishments in the neighborhood. Maria "Miss Mary" and Enrico Velleggia opened what was then called Friendly Tavern in 1937. Over time the couple purchased adjacent properties, expanding the restaurant, and renaming it Velleggia's. Mr. Velleggia was not a cook, so he stuck to the business side, while Miss Mary, using her own family recipes, made everything from scratch.

Sometime during the late '40s the restaurant became the "unofficial office" of the late mayor, Thomas J. D'Alesandro, and later his son, Thomas J. D'Alesandro III who would also become mayor of Baltimore. Visiting celebrities included Danny DeVito and baseball legend, Joe DiMaggio. Mae West dined at Velleggia's following her appearances at Ford's Theatre, and always brought Miss Mary a corsage.

The Velleggia's son, Frank took over the restaurant in 1990. Miss Mary remained in command of the kitchen until about 1993 when (at the age of 86) she turned those duties over to her grandson, Rick Velleggia. Her advice: "Cook for the people like your cooking for your family and everything will be fine."

"Little Italy Open Air Film Festival" by muralist Marshall Adams located at the corner of Pratt/High Streets.

Saltimbocca alla Romana

A "signature" house classic. Chicken or turkey breast may be substituted for veal, if preferred.

Serves: 6

+ **2 pounds** veal scaloppine or 6 large slices
+ **12** thin slices prosciutto ham
+ **12** thin slices mozzarella cheese
+ **3 tablespoons** olive oil
+ **2 tablespoons** butter
+ Flour
+ **½ cup** onions, very finely chopped
+ **¾ cup** dry Marsala
+ **½ cup** chicken stock
+ Salt and pepper to taste

With a flat mallet, pound the meat to make thin slices about 8" by 4 ½". If using small scaloppini, pound 2 or 3 together to make larger size. Place ham and cheese over scaloppini to almost completely cover each slice. Bring the bottom up to the middle and the top down and over like an envelope. Pound the ends together. (This can be done up to a day ahead).

Heat together the olive oil and butter. Dust the veal packages lightly with flour and quickly sauté. When they are golden brown on one side, flip them over and add the chopped onions to the skillet. Toward the end of browning completely, add the Marsala and stock to the pan and cook through. Transfer the scaloppini to a warmed serving plate. Reduce the sauce, if necessary. Season with salt and pepper and pour sauce over veal. Serve immediately.

Adapted from: Dining in - Baltimore by Bonnie Rapoport

Macheroni alla Pescatore

An intensely flavored seafood pasta in a spicy tomato sauce. Buon appetito!!

Serves: 4

+ **½ cup each:** dry white wine, water
+ **1** medium onion, finely chopped (about **1 ½** cups)
+ **12 each**, in the shell: mussels, clams, well-scrubbed
+ **1 tablespoon** extra-virgin olive oil
+ **4** cloves garlic, thinly sliced
+ **1 can** (28 ounces) crushed tomatoes
+ **¼ cup** dry sherry
+ **1 ½ teaspoon** dried oregano

+ **¼ cup** chopped fresh basil
+ **¼ teaspoon each**, salt, freshly ground black pepper
+ **⅛ teaspoon** crushed red pepper flakes
+ **8** raw medium shrimp, peeled and deveined
+ **¾ pound** calamari (squid), cleaned and sliced
+ **12 ounces** dried pasta (your favorite shape), cooked

Combine the wine, water, and ¼ cup of the onion in a large pot. Bring to a boil, reduce heat, and simmer 5 minutes. Add the mussels and clams, cover tightly, and steam until opened, about 3 to 5 minutes. Remove from heat and set aside.

Heat the oil and garlic in a skillet until the garlic starts to sizzle. Add the remaining onion and cook covered, over low heat until translucent, about 15 minutes. Add tomatoes, sherry, oregano, basil, salt, pepper, and red pepper flakes. Simmer for 10 minutes, uncovered.

Add the calamari to the tomato sauce and cook for 2 minutes. Add the shrimp, the mussels, and clams along with their cooking liquid. Mix well and continue to cook until the shrimp turn pink and opaque, about 2 more minutes. Do NOT overcook. Serve over your favorite pasta.

Adapted From: The Chicago Tribune, by Jeanne Jones, June 10, 1993

Shrimp Scampi

The garlicky goodness of the scampi sauce beckons for warm, crusty bread served alongside a fresh, garden green salad.

Serves: 2

+ **12** large raw shrimp
+ **1** cup butter
+ **6 to 7** garlic cloves, cut in half
+ White wine to taste
+ **1 tablespoon** lemon juice

+ **⅛ teaspoon** red pepper
+ **⅛ teaspoon** oregano
+ **⅛ teaspoon** salt
+ **⅛ teaspoon** pepper

Place all ingredients in a skillet. Cook about 6 minutes or until shrimp appear opaque. Serve over rice or linguini.

Adapted from: Beyond Beer and Crabs by Maryland Chapter Arthritis Foundation

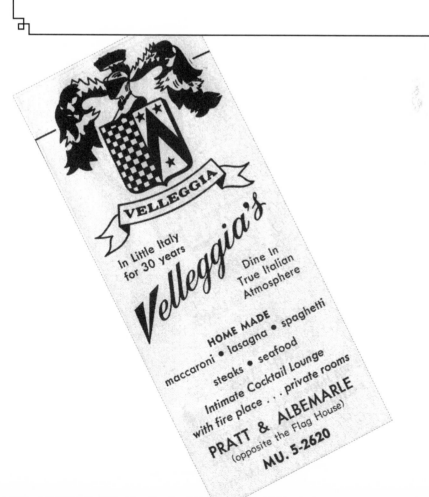

Downtown Baltimore (formerly Chinatown)

Martick's Restaurant Francaise
214 West Mulberry Street

1970 - 2008

Morris "Mo" Martick was born in the house that would become Martick's restaurant at 214 West Mulberry Street. To his mix of bohemian and blue-collar customers Martick was known as a loveable eccentric. The restaurant began as a grocery store run by Martick's parents and it later became a speakeasy during Prohibition. In 1933, following Repeal, his parents obtained one of the city's first liquor licenses, and opened a tavern. Typical bar fare was served until 1967 when Martick, taking over for his deceased mother, closed the tavern and set off for Paris to learn French cooking.

From Paris he made his way to a small country restaurant in Pacy-sur-Eure where he was advised to "keep everything as simple as possible, use fresh ingredients, don't overcook, and pay attention to the nuances." Inevitably he returned home inspired by his time away, and he soon opened the legendary Martick's Restaurant Francaise. The place became popular due, in part, to the inexpensive cuisine and shabby chic (before the term was coined) décor. He decorated the former tavern in snakeskin wallpaper and B-52 fuselage aluminum!

Martick's, located in a rather seedy appearing house with no signage or windows, certainly did not appear to be a restaurant. It probably would have had even more fans if they'd only been able to find the place. In addition, it wasn't located in the best of neighborhoods. To get in one approached a locked blue door with a secret doorbell that dated back to its speakeasy days. Assuming he could accommodate you, Martick would check you out through the peephole before buzzing you in.

The menus were always handwritten and photocopied. Martick never used a written recipe - they were all in his head. The kitchen turned out customer favorites like bouillabaisse, sweet potato soup, and beef Burgundy until Martick's retirement in 2008.

Morris Martick's World's Best Sweet Potato Soup

The Baltimore Sun ran this recipe in Morris Martick's own words in a 2006 food section story. Martick preferred to improvise and never used a written recipe.

Serves: 4

Boil 4 sweet potatoes until tender. Remove skin. Cut into large cubes. Put into saucepan, then add:

- Diced carrots (matchstick size), broccoli, string beans, mushrooms
- "A little bit of water." (We added about 1 ½ cups)
- Brown sugar (tablespoon per serving)
- "An appropriate amount" of butter (tablespoon per serving)
- Heavy whipping cream (How much? Use your instincts as a cook)

Bring to a boil and simmer until vegetables are cooked through (potatoes should be smooth) and soup is slightly thickened.

Don't overcook. "Or the cream will curdle."

(Note: We tested Martick's recipe using 4 sweet potatoes, 2 cups shredded carrots, 2 ½ cups broccoli florets, 2 ½ cups string beans, 2 cups sliced mushrooms, 4 tablespoons brown sugar, 4 tablespoons butter and ¾ cup heavy cream.)

Source: The Baltimore Sun, Glen Fawcett, December 12, 2006

Charles Center

Maison Marconi
106 West Saratoga Street

1920 – 2005

*M*aison Marconi, a.k.a. Marconi's, was a refined, genteel Baltimore institution founded by Chef Fiorenzo Bo. Bo was born in Turin, Italy and began his career as a cook at Claridge's in London. He was later associated with several restaurants in New York before opening Maison Marconi's. Bo named the restaurant after the Italian inventor, Guglielmo Marconi.

John C. Brooks started as a waiter in 1926 and eventually bought Marconi's from Bo in 1947. He would work there until the Saturday before his death at age 89 in 1999. Brooks hired chef Antonio Sartori in 1956 and Sartori remained there for 42 years, 36 of them as chef. Since its 1920 opening, Marconi's had employed a total of only four head chefs!

The restaurant's cuisine was Continental, with both French and Italian. Over the years it was a favorite of H. L. Mencken, Sinclair Lewis, and bandleader, Fred Waring. The popular Italian chopped salad was assembled in the kitchen but chopped and mixed tableside in big wooden bowls by the most professional waiters. The house's signature dish was Lobster Cardinale made with sherry in a rich cream sauce. The Marconi kitchen's classic methods of cooking included Meuniere, Veronique, Bordelaise, and Bonne Femme. French vanilla ice cream enrobed in a dark chocolate ganache was a meal-ending tradition. The chocolate sauce was a closely guarded secret recipe and some wondered why there was anything else on the dessert menu.

Marconi's won the "America Classics" award from the James Beard Foundation for being one of four of the nation's "locally owned and operated regional restaurants that have withstood the test of time and are beloved in their communities." It was the kind of place where old-line Baltimore patrons still dressed for dinner and celebrated milestones. Silvio Passalacqua, an 88-year-old kitchen helper recalled that the ultimate accolade came when a convicted murderer, condemned to hang at the Maryland Penitentiary, requested a plate of spaghetti from Marconi's for his final meal.

In 2000, Peter Angelos, attorney and owner of the Baltimore Orioles, purchased Marconi's. His intention was to relocate the restaurant to one of his Charles Street projects in the central business district. This never materialized, and Marconi's closed in 2005 to the dismay of many old guard loyalists who still miss both the rituals and their favorite dishes.

Italian Chopped Salad

Marconi's never officially published or shared any recipes. This inspired version is credited to Andi of Long Meadow Farm who was well acquainted with Marconi's famous chopped salad.

Serves: 4 to 6

+ 1 medium head iceberg lettuce, torn
+ 2 hard-boiled eggs, quartered
+ 1 large tomato (Roma or plum tomato)
+ 1 (2-ounce) can anchovies packed in oil, drained and chopped (optional)

+ ½ small onion, chopped finely
+ 1 stalk celery, chopped
+ ¼ teaspoon fresh ground pepper
+ ½ cup mayonnaise (low-fat can be used)
+ ¼ cup sweet peas (fresh or frozen; optional)

After chilling, mix together lettuce, eggs, tomato, anchovies, onion, celery, and pepper in a large chilled salad bowl. Add mayonnaise and toss completely. Using two knives, chop salad thoroughly. Add peas, if desired.

Plate on individual salad plates with crackers for scooping.

Adapted from: The Baltimore Sun, Julie Rothman, October 18, 2003

Lobster Cardinale

Making its debut at the restaurant in 1930, Lobster Cardinale was probably Marconi's most famous dish and definitely one of its most popular.

Serves: 4

+ **4** 1-pound lobsters
+ **4 tablespoons** butter
+ **8 ounces** white mushrooms, sliced
+ **1** shallot, minced
+ Salt and freshly ground white pepper to taste
+ **3** egg yolks
+ **1 cup** heavy cream
+ **2 tablespoons** La Ina or other fino sherry
+ **1 tablespoon** fresh parsley leaves, minced
+ **1 tablespoon** fresh thyme leaves, minced

Cook lobsters in a large pot of boiling water over high heat for 15 minutes. Drain. When cool enough to handle, remove meat from shells, leaving tails and heads intact. Cut meat into chunks and set aside. Using kitchen shears cut a 2"x 4" rectangular opening in backs of lobster tails.

Melt butter in a large heavy saucepan over medium-low heat. Add mushrooms and shallots, season with salt and pepper, and sauté until soft, about 10 minutes. To keep warm, set saucepan over a larger pan of simmering water over medium-low heat.

Lightly whisk egg yolks in a mixing bowl, whisking in cream. Add sherry, parsley, thyme, and lobster, then add to mushrooms in saucepan, stirring constantly with a wooden spoon until thickened, about 10-15 minutes. Adjust seasonings to taste and serve in lobster shells. Garnish with parsley and lemon wedges.

Adapted from: www.saveur.com, April 11, 2007

Chocolate Ganache

Inspired by Marconi's. The secret, as they say, is in the sauce.

Serves: 4

+ **8 ounces** high-quality bittersweet chocolate, coarsely chopped
+ **1 cup** heavy cream
+ **1 tablespoon** dark rum, Frangelico or Grand Marnier (optional)
+ **1-pint** French vanilla ice cream

Bring heavy cream to a boil in a small sauce pan. Add chopped chocolate to cream, remove from heat, and stir until chocolate is melted. Add optional liquor. Serve immediately. If you need to rewarm, place over low heat until melted, careful not to bring to a boil.

Adapted from: www.baltimoremd.com, Cathy Adams

Marconi's
~ A Baltimore Tradition Since 1920~

106 W. Saratoga St.
410-727-9522
Tues-Sat 11:30-8:30
Complimentary Valet Parking after 5:00
Private Party Rooms Available

Charles Center

The Women's Industrial Exchange
333 North Charles Street

1880-2002

The Women's Industrial Exchange began after the Civil War as a non-profit organization where women could bring their handcrafts to be sold to local citizens and visitors. The first gatherings were held at the home of Mrs. G. Harmon Brown of Baltimore. The Women's Industrial Exchange was established as a way for women in need to earn a discreet living. At that time, it was frowned upon for a woman to work outside of the home. Their mission: To provide women in financial need with an avenue to earn income through the sale of quality handmade goods. The Exchange operated a tea room, bakery, and consignment shop to support their mission. To this day the Women's Exchange remains headquartered in their historic building at 333 North Charles Street. The building was listed on the National Register of Historic Places in 1978.

The lunchroom with its black-and-white tiled floor was known for being old-fashioned and opened for breakfast and lunch. It seated 121 and its menu comprised Maryland fare. Grand-motherly waitresses in pastel uniforms with crisp white aprons served the most popular dish, known as the Women's Industrial Exchange Original - a chicken salad platter with tomato aspic and deviled eggs. One of the waitresses, Marguerite Schertle, worked at the Exchange until she was 95! The lunch room was used to shoot a scene in the movie *Sleepless in Seattle*. The director, Nora Ephron, cast Marguerite in a scene serving Annie (Meg Ryan) and her best friend, Becky (Rosie O'Donnell). When she tried to give Schertle some direction, Schertle responded, "Look, just let me do it my way." At that point, she'd been an employee for 45 years and knew her job well.

The Women's Industrial Exchange ceased operating in 2002, but in 2011 chef Irene Smith reopened the space as the Women's Industrial Kitchen which later closed in 2014.

Tomato Aspic

A very popular offering at the Exchange was the luncheon trio of tomato aspic, chicken salad, and deviled eggs.

Serves: 8

+ **4 cups** tomato juice
+ **1** small yellow onion, chopped
+ **2 stalks** celery, chopped
+ **6 sprigs** parsley
+ Juice of ½ lemon
+ **1 tablespoon** sugar

+ **1** bay leaf
+ **3** whole cloves
+ Pinch salt
+ **4** black peppercorns
+ **2 tablespoons** gelatin

Combine tomato juice, onions, celery, parsley, lemon juice, sugar, bay leaf, cloves, and peppercorns in a pot and bring to a boil. Reduce heat to low and simmer 30 to 40 minutes.

Dissolve gelatin in a ½ cup water. Strain juice mixture, discarding solids and return to pot adding in gelatin/water until dissolved. Pour into a lightly oiled 8" x 8" pan or ring mold, cover with plastic wrap, and chill until firm, about 4 hours. Serve with mayonnaise, if desired.

Adapted from: www.saveur.com

Chicken Salad

Serves: 10

+ **12** pieces boneless, skinless chicken breast
+ **1 ½ cups** celery, finely chopped
+ **2 cups** heavy mayonnaise

+ Lemon pepper seasoning
+ Salt and pepper to taste

Season chicken breasts lightly with lemon pepper seasoning. Bake breasts in oven for 30 minutes. Remove from oven and allow to cool. Cut into chunks, add finely chopped celery, and fold in mayonnaise, salt, and pepper. Chill salad for 3 to 4 hours before serving.

Note: If using a decorative tip, make sure it has a large enough opening to accommodate the addition of sweet pickle relish.

Adapted from: Baltimore Style submitted by Exchange chef Rozz DuPree

Deviled Eggs

Serves: 8

+ **1 dozen** eggs
+ **3 tablespoons** sweet pickle relish
+ **2 teaspoons** honey mustard
+ **6 tablespoons** heavy mayonnaise
+ Salt and ground black pepper, to taste

Boil eggs on medium flame for approximately 20 minutes. Peel eggs under cold water, slice in half, and remove yolk. Mash yolks in a small bowl and combine with sweet pickle relish, honey mustard, and heavy mayonnaise. Add salt and pepper. Chill about two hours to allow the flavors to blend. Place mixture into a piping bag fitted with a decorative tip (see note) and fill the halved egg whites.

Placing a bed of mesclun lettuce on a dinner plate, arrange chicken salad in the middle. Cut the tomato aspic into small triangles and surround the chicken salad. Add deviled eggs. Serve with a dinner roll, butter, and your favorite salad dressing.

Note: If using a decorative tip, make sure it has a large enough opening to accommodate the addition of sweet pickle relish.

Adapted from: Baltimore Style submitted by Exchange chef Rozz DuPree

Charlotte Russe

This old-fashioned European dessert was invented by the French chef, Marie-Antoine Careme (1784-1833). It is a chilled cake that pairs fruit, Bavarian cream, and lady fingers and is perfect for a special occasion celebration.

Serves: 8

Ladyfingers:
+ **½ cup** unsalted butter
+ **1 cup** white sugar
+ **½ cup** heavy whipping cream
+ **1 tablespoon** vanilla extract
+ **1 ¾ cups** all-purpose flour
+ **½ teaspoons** baking powder

Filling:
+ **⅓ cup** unflavored gelatin powder
+ **¼ cup** milk, at room temperature
+ **2 ½ cups** heavy cream
+ **1 ½ cups** sugar
+ **2 tablespoons** vanilla extract
+ **7** egg whites

Assembly:
+ Fresh berries, for topping

Ladyfingers:

Cream the butter, sugar, cream, and vanilla until fluffy and light.

Sift the flour and baking powder together. Add the flour mixture to the creamed butter with a spatula. Mix slowly until totally incorporated. Refrigerate 1 hour.

Preheat oven to 350°.

Place the batter in a pastry bag fitted with a ½" plain round tip. Alternately, use a plastic bag, cutting a corner off, leaving a ½" opening.

Line a cookie sheet with parchment paper. Pipe batter onto paper in six ½" x 5" strips. Grease a 9" x 2" round baking pan and squeeze the remaining batter into it.

Place both pans in the preheated oven and bake about 10 to 15 minutes, until the fingers are golden brown and spring back lightly when touched. Remove from oven and allow to cool completely.

Cut the ladyfingers in half. Each piece should measure about 2" x 2 ½".

Charlotte Russe (cont'd)

Filling:

Sprinkle the gelatin into a bowl. Add the milk and stir gently until the gelatin is absorbed and appears granular.

Beat the cream and sugar together until stiff. Add the vanilla and beat an additional 3 minutes. Add the gelatin and milk mixture and beat an additional 5 minutes.

In a separate bowl, beat the egg whites until slightly stiff peaks form. Fold the egg whites gently into the whipped cream mixture.

For assembly: Set out a 9" springform pan or line a 9" cake pan with foil, so the foil sticks up above the pan and forms handles.

Place the round cake layer in the bottom of the prepared pan. Arrange the ladyfingers in a ring around the edge of the pan, rounded side out. Gently pour the mixture of cream and egg whites into the pan carefully, so as not to knock over any ladyfingers. Smooth the top over with a spatula. Arrange berries decoratively around top.

To completely set, chill for at least 12 hours.

Remove the collar from the springform pan and cut the cake into slices. If using a foil-lined pan, another set of hands will be helpful to hold the pan steady as you lift the cake out by the handles.

Adapted from: Baltimore Chef's Table by Kathy Wielech Patterson and Neal Patterson

Mount Vernon

The Brass Elephant
924 North Charles Street
1980-2009

*L*ocated in a 19th century Victorian row house, The Brass Elephant was an architectural showplace that epitomized Old World elegance. Once a part of the huge Belvedere estate owned by John Eager Howard, a portion of the property went to his son, Benjamin Chew Howard, who built the home around 1850. By the 1860s the mansion was owned by Charles Morton Stewart, a Brazilian coffee importer. He purchased it as a winter residence for his wife and 14 children. The third owner was a local merchant, George Wroth Knapp, Jr. He and his wife, Sarah Gilfrey, used the mansion as a second home. Knapp, a trader who traveled extensively through China and India, had acquired carved teak collections and elephant sconces as ornamental décor. The couple invested about $100,000 on Rinehart marble mantles, Tiffany stained glass and Waterford crystal chandeliers, pieces whose value amounts to millions today.

Eventually this section of Charles Street became less desirable as a place for residences. Around 1930 Potthast Brothers Furniture moved into the building, converting the space into a stunning showroom. By the '70s Potthast had closed for business and some investors including William Paley, Jr., the son of William S. Paley of CBS fame, opened The Brass Elephant restaurant. Unfortunately, the restaurant was foreclosed on, but in 1980 Jack Elsby and Randy Stahl bought the building at auction, and The Brass Elephant went on to flourish for nearly thirty years.

The main dining room and multiple smaller rooms occupied the main floor. Each dining room was impossibly resplendent with exquisitely carved fireplace mantles and carved teak accents. Upstairs was the beautiful Tusk Lounge, with its Waterford crystal chandelier, and a ceiling painted like a cloudy sky. The overall design seemed to suggest a nostalgia for Baltimore's fine dining past. I can see why it was my mother's favorite 'special occasion' restaurant, or anyone else's for that matter.

The cuisine was northern Italian and Continental prepared with a French tendency. The restaurant won the Wine Spectator Award and several DiRoNA awards. *Baltimore Magazine* voted the Brass Elephant "the best place in Baltimore to wear a slinky black dress." Ultimately the restaurant fell on hard times and closed in 2009.

Linda and Steven Revelis purchased the building in 2015 and began renovations, bringing the property up to date. In 2016 the Revelises, who dated, and were married at the Brass Elephant, wanted to pay homage and re-opened the doors to their own dream restaurant, The Elephant.

Seafood Gazpacho

This refreshing gazpacho makes a perfect warm weather meal and encourages me to frequent my local farmer's market during the summer months.

Serves: 10 to 12

+ **2 ½** English cucumbers, peeled and quartered
+ **2** large tomatoes, quartered and seeded
+ **½** green pepper, quartered and seeded
+ **¼** red onion, sliced
+ **¼ cup** tequila
+ **4** scallions
+ **½ teaspoon** garlic, minced

+ **8 cups** tomato juice
+ **¼ cup** red wine vinegar
+ **½ tablespoon** cumin
+ **½ tablespoon** white pepper
+ **4 drops** Tabasco sauce
+ **1 tablespoon** kosher salt
+ **1-pound** jumbo lump crabmeat, picked

Warm tequila in a small saucepan to burn off the alcohol, being careful not to flame. In a food processor, place the cucumbers, tomatoes, peppers, onions, scallions, garlic, tequila, and tomato juice. Puree, but do not liquefy - you want some chunks. In a large bowl, combine chopped vegetable mixture with the red wine, cumin, white pepper, Tabasco sauce, and salt. Stir to combine well and chill for at least 1 hour. Garnish with lump crabmeat.

Adapted from: A Taste of Maryland History by Debbie Nunley

Eggplant Manicotti

This elegant dish is worth the extra time and effort it takes to prepare the crepes from scratch, but if short on time you can substitute a box of manicotti or cannelloni pasta. Either way, it's a tasty showstopper!

Yield: 10 crepes

+ 3 eggs
+ 1 ¼ **cups** whole milk
+ **4 to 5 tablespoons** butter, melted, divided
+ ½ **cups** flour, sifted
+ Pinch of salt
+ Pinch of mixed herbs

+ 3 eggplants
+ 1 shallot, diced and sautéed in oil
+ **2 tablespoons** ricotta cheese, plus extra for garnish
+ **1 tablespoon** basil
+ Salt and pepper to taste
+ Tomato sauce

Preheat oven to 350°.

In a medium bowl, whisk together eggs, milk, and 1 tablespoon butter. Add in flour, salt, and herbs mixing until lump-free. Heat a small nonstick pan and add a small amount of butter. Add 2 tablespoons batter. Cook on one side, then slide out of pan onto wax paper. Mixture should make 10 crepes.

Cut eggplants in half and score insides. Lay cut side down in a shallow baking dish. Add 2 cups water to dish and bake for about 30 minutes until eggplants are soft. Remove from oven, drain, and allow to cool. Scoop out cooked eggplant flesh and place in a medium bowl. Add shallots, 2 tablespoons ricotta, and basil. Stir to combine. Add salt and pepper. Place about ¼ cup eggplant mixture on each crepe. Roll crepes and place in a rectangular baking dish. Bake for 10 minutes. Top each with a dollop of ricotta and serve with tomato sauce.

Adapted from: A Taste of Maryland History by Debbie Nunley

Brass Elephant's Paella Parellada

This version of "Rich Man's Rice" is a Catalan classic. I was fortunate enough to experience Paella Parellada at the venerable 7 Portes Restaurant in Barcelona and can attest to this version's authenticity. The trick here is easy; just begin with the freshest of ingredients. Deliciós!!

Serves: 2-3

+ **⅛ teaspoon** saffron threads
+ **2 tablespoons** olive oil
+ **½ cup** onions, diced
+ **2 tablespoons** garlic, chopped
+ **½ cup** red peppers, diced
+ **½ cup** chorizo sausage, cut bite-size
+ **4 ounces** boneless, skinless chicken, coarse chopped
+ **½ teaspoon** paprika or cayenne
+ Salt and pepper to taste
+ **½ cup** tomatoes, diced

+ **2 tablespoons** parsley, chopped
+ **1 ½ cups** cooked rice
+ **3 ½ cups** chicken stock (home-made or commercial)
+ **4** cockle clams or other clams, cleaned
+ **4 ounces** ocean fish
+ **4** mussels, cleaned
+ **4** shrimp (16/20 count), cleaned and deveined
+ **½ cup** white wine
+ **½ cup** haricot verts (baby French green beans)

Begin by toasting saffron lightly, mash into a powder, and set aside. Heat oil on medium-high in a large skillet with a tight-fitting lid. Add onions, garlic, and red peppers and sauté until onions are transparent.

In a separate pan, sauté chorizo sausage and drain well. To the onion/pepper mixture, add chicken, sausage, paprika, salt, and pepper and sauté until chicken begins to brown. Reduce heat to simmer and quickly stir in tomatoes, parsley, and rice. Add chicken stock and saffron, stirring to combine. Lower heat and cover. When rice absorbs 2/3 of the stock (after about 20 minutes), add clams and cover for about 5 minutes. Stir in ocean fish, mussels, and shrimp. Re-cover and let simmer for 5 minutes. Add wine and haricot verts. Cook uncovered until seafood is done discarding any shells that did not open.

Adapted from: Maryland's Historic Restaurants by Dawn O'Brien and Rebecca Schenck

Brass Elephant's Mac and Cheese

This recipe for creamy baked comfort-food goodness is easily customized by using any types of cheeses that you enjoy.

Serves: 8 to 10

- ✢ **4 tablespoons** butter *
- ✢ **4 tablespoons** flour *
- ✢ **1-quart** milk
- ✢ ¼ yellow onion, halved
- ✢ 1 bay leaf
- ✢ 2 cloves
- ✢ **½ pound** white cheddar, grated
- ✢ **½ pound** Gruyere, grated
- ✢ **½ pound** fontina, grated
- ✢ Pinch of salt
- ✢ **1 ½ teaspoons** nutmeg
- ✢ **1 teaspoon** white pepper
- ✢ White truffle oil
- ✢ **1-pound** pasta

Preheat oven to 400°.

Bring a stock pot of salted water to a boil. Add your favorite pasta to water. When pasta is al dente, drain and cool. Heat milk in a medium saucepan along with onion, cloves, and bay leaf. In a separate large saucepan, melt butter and combine with flour over medium heat, stirring constantly until mixture is a smooth roux. Add the milk in a steady stream, stirring constantly until the sauce is smooth and thickened. Add grated cheeses. Season with nutmeg, salt, and pepper. Strain cheese sauce before adding the pasta. Pour in a baking dish and drizzle with white truffle oil. Bake for about 30 minutes or until golden brown and bubbly.

*A cheese sauce prepared from a roux typically forms the basis for macaroni and cheese. I have taken the liberty of including that here.

Adapted from: Baltimore Style, September/October 2006

THE BRASS ELEPHANT

924 N. Charles St.
Baltimore, Md.

Brass Elephant's Dried Fruit Compote with Mascarpone and Brown Sugar Glaze

This recipe makes a lot but can easily enough be halved. The dried fruit compote on its own makes a delicious topping for French toast or waffles.

Serves: 10-12

Fruit Compote:
+ **2 cups** sugar
+ **1 cup** water
+ Juice of 1 lemon
+ ⅓ cup honey
+ **2** cinnamon sticks
+ Freshly ground black pepper to taste
+ **4 pounds** dried fruit (apricots, raisins, dates, cranberries, and cherries), chopped coarsely

+ **2 tablespoons** cornstarch
+ **1 cup** cold water

Mascarpone and Brown Sugar Glaze:
+ **½ cup** sugar
+ **1-pound** Mascarpone cheese, room temperature
+ **2 tablespoons** vanilla
+ **2 tablespoons** Grand Marnier
+ **1 to 2 tablespoons** brown sugar

Fruit Compote:
Place first 6 ingredients in a small saucepan and bring to a boil. Lower heat and let cook until mixture reaches the syrup stage. Strain syrup into a large pot and stir in dried fruit. Simmer for 10 minutes. Dissolve cornstarch in water and stir into fruit mixture. Raise heat and stir until mixture reaches boiling; reduce heat and simmer until thickened.

Glaze:
Place white sugar and cheese in a bowl and beat until smooth; add vanilla and Grand Marnier.

To assemble, pour fruit mixture into a lightly greased ramekin or casserole and top with cheese mixture. Sprinkle with brown sugar and place under a broiler until sugar becomes glazed and bubbly. Serve immediately.

Adapted from: Maryland's Historic Restaurants by Dawn O'Brien and Rebecca Schenck

Mount Vernon

Louie's Bookstore and Café
518 North Charles Street

1981-1999

For many, Louie's was the cool-hipster place to be. What could be a better way to end a late night than with coffee, a slice of decadent cheesecake and a jazz trio? Louie's was an artistic enterprise and had a relaxed feel about it. The main purpose of the Café was to provide employment for artists and musicians. Artists exhibited their paintings, hanging them on the sponge-painted red walls. Known for its rather indifferent staff, the arts were always priority. Even with the sometimes-flaky service, customers had a fondness for the place, and chalked up any imperfections to support for the artistic community. Louie's was listed on Oprah's Favorite Things (in Baltimore).

Artist Jimmy Rouse purchased the Café in 1981 from Kramer Books and named it for his then 6-year-old son. He opened Louie's as a literary bookstore with a two-level dining room in the rear. Chicken Chestertown became its signature dish, a recipe handed down from his father, developer James Rouse, who had grown up on the Eastern Shore. The Café also had some of the best ice cream and dessert selections offered in Baltimore. Rouse decided to sell the operation in 1999 so that he could work full-time as both a painter and community activist.

louie's
the
bookstore
café

"baltimore's
best brunch"
city paper, 1995

518 n.charles st.
baltimore, md
21201

bookstore
410.962.1222
café
410.962.1224
fax
410.962.8959

Chicken Chestertown

This recipe is a Rouse family dish borrowing its name from nearby Chestertown. According to a former cook at Louie's, the chicken is best marinated for at least 24 hours for the flavors to fully develop. Alternately, it may be grilled which helps to seal in the juices resulting in a moist and tender chicken.

Serves: 3-4

+ **1** chicken, 1 ½ to 2 pounds
+ **1 teaspoon** ginger
+ **2 teaspoon** curry
+ **1 tablespoon** chili powder
+ Juice of 4 lemons
+ **2** garlic cloves, crushed
+ **1** onion, chopped
+ **1 teaspoon** salt
+ **8 tablespoons** olive oil

Preheat oven to 350°.

Quarter the chicken or cut it up into individual pieces. Set aside. Prepare marinade by mixing ginger, curry, chili powder, lemon juice, garlic cloves, onion, and salt. Whisk in the olive oil. If necessary, add a little more for consistency. Pour marinade into a shallow pan and add chicken parts. Marinate 4 hours at room temperature or cover pan with a damp tea towel and refrigerate overnight.

Bake covered with foil for about 45 minutes, basting occasionally. Remove foil and continue baking 10 more minutes or until golden brown.

Adapted from: The Baltimore Sun, May 29, 1988

Black Bottom Pie

This old-fashioned pie is a chocolate lover's delight! A nod to the American south, it represents the lowlands along the Mississippi River.

Yield: 1 pie (9-inch)

+ **1** 9-inch baked pie shell
+ **1 cup** heated milk
+ **4** eggs, separated
+ **1 tablespoon** cornstarch
+ **1 cup** sugar
+ Dash salt
+ **1** envelope unflavored gelatin

+ **¼ cup** water
+ **2 ounces** unsweetened chocolate
+ **1 teaspoon** vanilla
+ **¼ teaspoon** cream of tartar
+ **2 tablespoons** rum
+ Whipped cream
+ Shaved unsweetened chocolate

Combine milk and beaten egg yolks in a double boiler. Add cornstarch, ¾ cup sugar, and salt. Cook on low heat about 15 minutes or until thick. In a bowl dissolve gelatin in water. Stir in hot custard mixture and place in refrigerator until chilled, but not set.

In another bowl, combine 1 ¼ cups of custard, melted chocolate, and vanilla. Pour into pie shell. Next, combine egg whites, cream of tartar, and remaining sugar, beating completely. Stir in the remaining custard. Blend in rum. Pour into pie shell and chill until set and ready to serve. Top with whipped cream and shaved chocolate.

Adapted from: The Evening Sun, October 20, 1983

Mount Vernon

John Eager Howard Room
The Belvedere Hotel
1 East Chase Street

1903-1991

The Belvedere Hotel was built on property that was once part of the vast estate of General John Eager Howard, hero of the American Revolution and Governor of Maryland. The Howard mansion, Belvedere, was constructed in 1794, approximately one block east of the existing hotel. Taking its name from the nearby site, the Hotel is a magnificent example of Beaux Art design. It served as the headquarters for the 1912 Democratic National Convention that nominated Woodrow Wilson.

During Prohibition the John Eager Room, located off the lobby, was known simply as the "Tea Room." Afternoon tea was served daily to Baltimore's nobility. Wallis Warfield, (later the Duchess of Windsor) a Baltimore native, was a regular at these teas. Following Prohibition, it continued to be a preferred meeting place for afternoon tea, and for cocktails, both before and after dinner. Guests often enjoyed listening to a quartet of musicians.

In 1976 the Hotel was purchased by Victor Frenkil, a Baltimore businessman, and restoration of the property began.

The impressive John Eager Howard Room was one of the most beautiful restaurants in Baltimore. The Room is preserved by the Maryland Historical Trust, and features an exquisite original carved marble fireplace, and five original crystal chandeliers. The walls are decorated by hand-painted murals on Japanese rice paper depicting turn-of-the-century (19th-20th) Baltimore. My first dinner at the John Eager Howard Room was with my family at my grandmother's invitation. The setting was pure Old-World glamour I don't believe I had ever witnessed before. Upon entering the elegant dining room, we were greeted with displays of fresh white flowers and soft melodies from a grand piano. The menu, for the most part, was Continental cuisine, along with Baltimore seafood specialties. Both food and service were excellent. While I honestly can't remember what I selected for my entree that night, I will always cherish the memory of that splendid evening my very generous grandmother chose to share with us.

Lobster Bisque

Authentic lobster bisque is flavored with the shells, and when pureed they serve as a thickener. This satisfying recipe from the John Eager Howard Room is no different.

Serves: 6

+ **10** chicken lobster bodies (not tails or claws)
+ **4** carrots, coarsely chopped
+ **3** onions, coarsely chopped
+ **3 to 4 stalks** celery, coarsely chopped
+ **8 to 10 cloves** of garlic, chopped
+ **4** bay leaves
+ **1 to 1 ½ cups** butter

+ **1 cup** flour (approximately)
+ **4 small cans** tomato puree; **8 cups** water
+ Salt and pepper to taste
+ **1-ounce** brandy and **1-ounce** sherry
+ **½ cup** heavy cream
+ Cooked chopped shrimp or lobster meat for garnish

Cook the lobster bodies, carrots, onions, celery, garlic, and bay leaves in the butter in a large skillet over direct heat, covered, for 30 minutes or until the lobster is cooked. Everything should fit in one layer and be stirred frequently. (Alternately, melt butter in a roasting pan at 375°, add lobster bodies, vegetables, and seasonings and cook, covered, 30 minutes.)

Blend in flour to form a smooth roux and transfer everything to a large stockpot.

Add the tomato puree and water. Bring to a boil. Lower heat and reduce until there are only 6 cups left. Season with salt and pepper.

The shells will be very soft at this point, so everything can now be pureed in a blender or food processor. Return this puree to the pot. Depending on desired consistency, reduce if thin, or add water if too thick.

Add the brandy and the sherry. Blend in the heavy cream and return to a simmer. Taste and season with more salt and pepper if necessary. Transfer to individual handled soup bowls.

Sprinkle with cooked chopped shrimp or lobster meat as desired.

Adapted from: Dining In - Baltimore by Bonnie Rapoport

Crab Imperial

This intensely flavored version of crab imperial is a winner thanks to the addition of chives and capers.

Serves: 4

+ **1-pound** Maryland regular or backfin crabmeat, picked

+ **¼ cup** mayonnaise

+ **1 teaspoon** olive oil

+ **¼ cup** chopped chives or chopped onion top; chopped parsley with juice scraped from small dried onion

+ **1 tablespoon** lemon juice

+ **5 drops** oil from can of anchovies

+ **½ teaspoon** capers

+ **3 dashes** liquid hot pepper sauce

+ **3 dashes** Worcestershire sauce

+ Cracker crumbs or seasoned bread crumbs, for topping

+ Paprika, for topping

+ Butter, for topping

Preheat oven to 450°.

In a large bowl, combine the mayonnaise and olive oil. Add chives, lemon juice, anchovy oil, capers, hot pepper sauce, and Worcestershire sauce, mixing well. Add the crabmeat into mayonnaise mixture and mix gently.

Place the crab mixture into individual crab/scallop shells or casseroles. Top lightly with cracker or seasoned bread crumbs. Sprinkle with paprika and dot with butter.

Bake until brown and bubbly, about 10 minutes.

Adapted from: Maryland Seafood Cookbook II by the Maryland Department of Agriculture

Crème Caramel

Crème caramel or flan is easier to prepare in individual ramekins to avoid undercooking. This was an extremely popular dessert staple served in many European restaurants because it could be prepared well in advance and kept refrigerated. It is a variation on crème brûlée which requires the use of a small torch to caramelize the top.

Serves: 6

+ **2 ½ cups** milk
+ ¼ **cups** plus 2 tablespoons sugar
+ **3** cinnamon sticks
+ Grated rind of 1 lemon
+ **7** eggs

Caramel:
+ **½ cup** water
+ **¾ cup** sugar

Preheat oven to 350°.

Place 2 cups milk, sugar, cinnamon, and lemon rind into a saucepan. Bring to a boil and remove from heat. In another pot, beat together the remaining ½ cup milk and eggs.

When the boiling milk has cooled, gradually whisk into the milk/egg mixture. Strain into a bowl.

Prepare the custard cups as directed below and allow to harden.

Ladle the strained milk mixture into the caramel-lined cups. Place the custard cups in a roasting or baking pan that is at least 2" deep. Add enough water to come halfway up the sides of the cups.

Bake 40 minutes or until the flans test done - a toothpick inserted into the middle of each custard should emerge clean. Remove from water and chill. (This can be prepared a day ahead of serving.)

When ready to serve, press the custard gently with your fingers to loosen the edges. Take a small dessert plate and place it on top of each flan cup and invert. The crème should slide out easily.

Caramel:
Heat the water and sugar in a heavy saucepan over low heat. Stir with a spoon to dissolve the sugar. Once dissolved, let it boil until the syrup has turned a deep amber brown; be careful not to burn.

Immediately pour about 2 tablespoons of the caramel into the bottom of six 4-to-5-ounce custard cups or oven-proof ramekins. The caramel should cover the surface of the cups.

Adapted from: Dining In - Baltimore by the Bonnie Rapoport

Mount Vernon

Danny's
Charles at Biddle Streets

1961-1991

anny Dickman was the driving force behind Baltimore's most renowned restaurant. The skeptics said it would never go over in a city where "epicurean" meant steamed crabs and draught beer, but Dickman's goal was "to upgrade the region's taste in food." And that he did. His use of the tagline "cuisine for the connoisseur" became synonymous with Danny's.

As a boy Dickman scooped ice cream at his father's confectionary shop, and he later went on to work at his brother Charlie's restaurant, Dickman's Colonial House. After he opened Danny's in 1961, Dickman would visit New York City's leading French restaurants with the notion of duplicating them in Baltimore. He insisted on the best ingredients and would have Scotch salmon flown in from the British Isles. He purchased his meat from the same distributors that supplied some of New York's best restaurants. Danny's earned the city's only four-star rating in the Mobil Travel guide. Along with those four-stars came the four dollar-signs symbol.

One of the house specialties was shad roe, and every spring a banner went up outside the restaurant with the phrase, "The Run Is On." Before entrées arrived at the table, diners anticipated plates of cottage cheese, huge, hot popovers, and dill pickles brought by an amiable waitress. Many items on the menu were prepared tableside.

By the mid-1980s reviewers were becoming critical. Trendier restaurants were opening, and heavy French food was falling out of favor. In 1991 Dickman sold the restaurant to his son and daughter-in-law. Shortly after, the couple became embroiled in a divorce and Danny's closed later that year.

Baked Shad Stuffed with Roe

Delicate Shad is a springtime tradition here in Maryland.
The spawning season is from about mid-April through early June.

Serves: 6

+ **1 to 4-pound** shad

+ **1 tablespoon** parsley, finely chopped

+ **1 tablespoon** shallots, chopped

+ **1 tablespoon** butter plus more for finishing

+ **½ cup** soft bread crumbs

+ Salt and pepper to taste

+ Flour seasoned with salt and pepper, for dusting

+ Dry white wine, for basting

+ Lemon for garnish

Preheat oven to 400°.

Split and bone the shad. Prepare a stuffing by scalding one pair of shad roe in salted, boiling water for about 2 minutes. Drain and split the roes, scraping out the eggs into a bowl. Add the parsley, shallots, butter, bread crumbs, and salt and pepper; mix thoroughly.

Stuff and tie the fish. Place the fish on an oiled baking sheet or shallow dish. Sprinkle with flour. Dot with plenty of butter and bake for 25-35 minutes or until fish is tender when a toothpick is inserted, basting with white wine. Serve fish on a platter and garnish with lemon.

Adapted from: The Evening Sun, April 29, 1976

Crabe en Chemise - Crab Crepes

It is best to make the Mornay sauce, Hollandaise sauce and crepes in advance, but if you aren't feeling that adventurous, these days the sauces are readily available at most grocery stores.

Serves: 4 to 6

+ **1-pound** Maryland backfin crabmeat
+ **¼ teaspoon** salt
+ **¼ teaspoon** pepper
+ **½ cup** dry sherry

+ **2 cups** Mornay sauce (recipe follows)
+ **5 tablespoons** Hollandaise sauce divided (recipe follows)
+ **1 cup** heavy cream, whipped
+ **6 10"** crepes (recipe follows)

Clean cartilage from crabmeat. In 2-quart saucepan, place crabmeat, salt, pepper ,and ¼ cup sherry. Simmer until crabmeat is heated through, about 5 minutes. Add 1 cup mornay sauce, 1½ tablespoons Hollandaise sauce, and half of the whipped cream. Heat slowly until mixture is hot, being careful not to bring it to a boil. Place crepes on a baking sheet. Put about 1/3 cup crab mixture in the middle of each crepe and roll up.

In 1-quart saucepan, mix the remaining sherry, Mornay sauce, Hollandaise sauce, and whipped cream. Warm gently, but do not boil. Pour enough sauce mixture over each crepe to cover. Put crepes under broiler until golden browned and beginning to bubble.

Serve crepes on heated plates with remaining sauce on the side.

Mornay sauce:
Makes: about 2 ½ cups

+ **¼ cup** butter or margarine
+ **¼ cup** flour
+ **2 cups** milk

+ **¼ cup** grated Parmesan cheese
+ **¼ cup** finely cut Swiss cheese
+ **2** egg yolks
+ **¼ cup** butter or margarine
+ Salt and pepper, to taste

Melt butter in medium saucepan. Slowly blend in flour. Gradually stir in milk and cook, stirring constantly, over medium heat until mixture comes to a boil and thickens. Reduce heat, add Parmesan and Swiss cheese, and stir until cheese melts. Remove from heat.

Just before serving, beat egg yolks lightly in small bowl. Gradually add small amounts of the hot milk mixture to the egg, stirring constantly, until bowl feels warm to the touch. Then slowly stir egg mixture into the milk mixture. Cut butter into small pieces and stir into sauce. Add salt and pepper to taste. Do not attempt to reheat sauce after adding the egg yolks or it will curdle.

Crabe en Chemise - Crab Crepes (cont'd)

Hollandaise sauce:
Makes about: 1 cup

+ **3** egg yolks
+ **½ cup** butter, melted
+ **2 tablespoons** lemon juice
+ **½ teaspoons** salt
+ Few grains of cayenne pepper

In bowl, beat egg yolks with wire whisk or wooden spoon until smooth, but not fluffy. Slowly beat in melted butter, a little at a time. Slowly stir in lemon juice, then salt and cayenne pepper.

Note: Sauce may be made in advance and refrigerated. Allow it to reach room temperature before using. If separation occurs upon standing, add a little hot water, a teaspoon at a time until smooth.

Crepes:
+ **½ cup** milk
+ **½ cup** water
+ **2** large eggs
+ **⅛** teaspoon salt
+ **1 tablespoon** vegetable oil
+ **¾ cup** flour

In a small bowl, whip together milk, water, eggs, salt, and oil; beat in flour. Let stand about an hour.

Heat a small fry pan (or 10" fry pan) and grease lightly with vegetable oil. Pour in just enough batter to cover the pan with a very thin layer, tilting pan evenly spread batter. Cook on one side; toss or turn with spatula and brown the other side. Cook the crepes one by one, stacking them between pieces of waxed paper.

Makes 12 crepes, about 5" in diameter (or 6 10" crepes).

Note: Crepes can be made in advance and refrigerated for a day or two or frozen for later use.

Adapted from: Maryland Seafood Cookbook II by the Maryland Department of Agriculture

Steak Diane

Who was Diane? She was ancient Rome's goddess of the hunt. It's likely that Steak Diane is some variation on a dish that was associated with game. I would imagine that with meat rations during World War II, post-war diners might have appreciated the tableside flambé presentation of Steak Diane. However, it was considered dated by 1980 as the art of tableside cooking went by the wayside.

Serves: 6

+ **½ pound** unsalted butter
+ **1 ½ pounds** mushrooms, sliced
+ **¼ cup** shallots, minced
+ **¼ cup** snipped fresh parsley
+ **¾ cup** dry Madeira
+ **1** small filet of beef (about 2 pounds), cut crosswise into 3/8"slices
+ **¼ cup** Cognac or brandy

+ **1 ½ cups** beef stock or broth
+ **1 tablespoon** beurre manie, (see note)
+ **6 tablespoons** Escoffier Sauce Robert
+ **1 tablespoon** Worcestershire sauce
+ Salt and pepper to taste

Heat butter in a large skillet over medium-high heat until hot; add mushrooms, shallots, and parsley. Sauté for a couple minutes or until the shallot is translucent. Stir in the Madeira. Push the mushrooms to one side of the pan and add the beef. Sauté, until medium-rare, about 3 minutes turning once.

Heat the Cognac and pour over meat. Ignite. When flame dies, add the stock. Remove beef and mushrooms to a platter and keep warm.

Add beurre manie into skillet and cook stirring constantly, until sauce thickens, about 2 minutes. Stir in Robert and Worcestershire sauces. Season with salt and pepper. Return beef and mushrooms to pan. Spoon sauce over. Serve.

Note: To make 1 tablespoon of beurre manie, mix together 1 ½ teaspoons each softened butter and all-purpose flour.

Escoffier Sauce Robert is made from a reduction of white wine, chopped onions cooked in butter, demi-glace and finished with Dijon mustard.

Adapted from: Dining In - Baltimore by Bonnie Rapoport

Sole Louis XV

My mother arranged a dinner party (including my friends) to celebrate my twenty-first birthday at Danny's. It was the only time I was ever there, and I remember lingering over this luscious Dover sole entrée like it was yesterday!

Serves: 4

+ **2** Dover sole filets (8 pieces)
+ **2 tablespoons** shallots, chopped
+ **2 cups** white wine
+ **2 cups** Béchamel sauce (see index)
+ **½ cup** water
+ **½ teaspoon** salt
+ **¼ teaspoon** pepper
+ **¼ cup** Hollandaise sauce (see index)
+ **¼ cup** heavy cream, whipped
+ **2 ounces** cooked lobster
+ **8** mushrooms, sliced

Heat a heavy skillet over medium-high heat. When hot, add the sole filets along with the shallots, salt, pepper, white wine, and water. Poach for 10 minutes.

Remove the fish from the sauce and put it in a serving pan. To the wine sauce, add the lobster meat and mushrooms. Cook for 5 minutes. Add the lobster and mushrooms to the sole. Keep hot.

Reduce the white wine and shallot sauce until there are about 2 tablespoons left. Add the Béchamel and Hollandaise sauces and whipped cream; whisking until smooth. Heat through and pour over the sole. Place the sauce-covered dish under the broiler to glaze it.

Adapted from: The Baltimore Sun, August 22, 1984

Salade Beatrice

Danny Dickman named this salad for the Mrs.

Serves: 6

+ **2 ounces** sliced raw mushrooms
+ **2 ounces** watercress
+ **2 ounces** endive
+ **4 tablespoons** olive oil
+ **1 tablespoon** red wine vinegar
+ **1 tablespoon** Dijon mustard
+ Salt and freshly ground pepper

In a wooden salad bowl, whisk together oil and vinegar. Add mustard, salt and pepper. Add the greens and mushrooms tossing lightly.

Adapted from: The Evening Sun, April 29, 1976

Station North

Chesapeake Restaurant
1701 North Charles Street

1933-1989

$\mathcal{B}$ altimoreans were first introduced to the concept of charcoal-grilled steaks by the Friedman family. Legend has it that in 1936 Sidney Friedman returned to Baltimore from Chicago by train, carrying a charcoal grill on his lap. Earlier in the week, he had visited Ray's Steakhouse and indulged in his first-ever charcoal-grilled steak. He knew immediately that he had to duplicate it, and asked the chefs how they prepared them, and what type of grill they used. The rest, as they say, is history.

The Chesapeake began as a lunch counter, opened in 1913 by Morris Friedman, Sidney's father. After the end of Prohibition, in 1933, Morris remodeled and turned the deli into The Chesapeake Restaurant. It was only a couple of blocks from Penn Station, so it was truly a prime location. In 1935, when Morris became ill, Sidney took over. Initially, The Chesapeake was known as an upscale Maryland seafood destination. Its popularity grew even more when Sidney began serving char-grilled steaks, with potatoes and a roll for 85 cents - not inexpensive at the time. He had the beef brought in from Chicago and ran the advertisement, "cut your steak with a fork, else tear up the check and walk out." By 1939 the restaurant had been awarded by famed food critic Duncan Hines and was considered one of the most expensive and exclusive in Baltimore.

In the 1950s Sidney's younger brother, Phillip "Penny," a recent graduate of Cornell's School of Hotel Administration, took over the operation. In 1961 he bought the neighboring restaurant, Hasslinger's and expanded The Chesapeake from 29 seats to 300! It was the place to be seen and heard, frequented by ad men, media, politicians, lawyers, and athletes. On a Friday night it was next to impossible to get a table unless you reserved well in advance. And, speaking of reservations, when you secured one you were presented with personally embossed matchbooks on arrival.

James Beard, "Dean of American Cookery" presented The Chesapeake with the Benson and Hedges Award, including the restaurant in his book, *Entertaining with Style: Recipes from Great American Restaurants*. The Chesapeake was one of only 32 of America's best restaurants asked to contribute a favorite recipe, and Crab Imperial Chesapeake was the selection. According to Sidney, The Chesapeake was the first restaurant to offer Baltimore the Caesar salad. "The first Caesar salad ever served in Baltimore was made and served by me - in The Chesapeake."

The restaurant's interior featured dark paneled walls, red leather-like banquettes, and candlelit tables set with white tablecloths and fresh flowers. The comfortable Lamplighter Room had a fireplace while the Pen and Quill Lounge was furnished with a piano. In the late '60s my grandparents took what was then our family of four to dinner there sometimes. I remember being utterly enchanted by the place, because I had never had dinner anywhere as nice, and I felt so grown up. The fact that we were treated like royalty was not lost on me. My younger sister Rebecca and I indulged in Shirley Temple drinks before our entrees arrived. The Chesapeake is where I had my very first Crab Imperial. It was a thrill for me to find the original recipe and it's still marvelous! Another memory that stands out is that this is where my grandfather, Harley, and my younger sister, Rebecca, began their own tradition of sharing a huge steamed lobster.

There was also the Babe Ruth Room, a shrine loaded with memorabilia. The Chesapeake experienced a devastating fire in 1974 that completely destroyed the second floor, including the Babe Ruth Room and all its contents. Sadly, that marked the beginning of the end for The Chesapeake. The enormous loans necessary for renovations resulted in the business declaring bankruptcy in 1983. By 1985, the restaurant had been sold at foreclosure to Robert Sapero, and after 50 years was no longer in the Friedman family. Sapero tried to breathe new life back into The Chesapeake, but ultimately failed and the property was abandoned by 1989.

Baked Stuffed Oysters Chesapeake

This signature dish uses a basic crab imperial topper to "dress up" otherwise unadorned oysters.

Serves: 6

+ **¼ cup** green pepper, finely diced
+ **1** small pimiento, finely diced
+ **1 teaspoon** English mustard
+ Salt and pepper to taste
+ **½ cup** mayonnaise (approximately)

+ **1** egg yolk, beaten
+ **1-pound** lump crab meat
+ **18** large oysters
+ Paprika to taste

Preheat oven to 350°.

In a bowl, mix together the diced pepper and pimiento. Add the dry mustard, salt, pepper, and ¼ cup of mayonnaise and mix well. Add just enough egg yolk to moisten the mixture.

Add the crab meat and mix by hand to avoid breaking up the lumps.

Equally divide the mixture among the oysters on the half shells. Place them on top of rock salt. Top with a thin layer of mayonnaise and sprinkle with paprika. Bake them for 5 minutes, then broil until tops are golden brown.

Adapted from: Dining In - Baltimore by Bonnie Rapoport

Crab Imperial Chesapeake

It was great then and it's great now! For me, this is a true Maryland indulgence that I will always associate with the Chesapeake Restaurant.

Serves: 8

+ **1** green pepper, finely chopped
+ **2** pimientos, finely chopped
+ **2** eggs
+ **1 cup** mayonnaise
+ **1 tablespoon** salt

+ **1 tablespoon** English mustard
+ **½ teaspoon** white pepper
+ **3 pounds** lump crab meat
+ Additional mayonnaise
+ Paprika

Preheat oven to 350°.

Using a large bowl, add the green pepper, pimiento, eggs, 1 cup mayonnaise, salt, mustard, and white pepper, mixing well. Using your hands, add the crab meat and combine taking care not to break the lumps. Distribute the mixture into 8 crab shells or individual ramekins, mounding gently. Spread a thin layer of mayonnaise over tops and sprinkle with paprika. Bake for about 15 to 18 minutes. The imperial can be served hot or chilled.

Note: To use crab shells, scrub them with a brush to remove any debris and place the shells in a large pot or heavy Dutch oven and cover with hot water. Add 1 teaspoon of baking soda to the water and bring to a boil. Lower heat to a simmer, covered. Simmer for 20 minutes. Drain and dry the shells. The shells can be stored and re-used by simmering with baking soda after each use.

Adapted from: Benson & Hedges presents Entertaining with Style

Teriyaki Steak Chesapeake

Marinating the steak adds so much flavor and helps tenderize it. The great part here is that the marinade does double duty as a flavor infuser and a sauce. Delish!

Serves: 6

+ **2** large sirloin steaks, 1" thick or 3 pounds beef tenderloin cut into cubes

+ Teriyaki sauce

+ **2 tablespoons** fresh ginger root, grated

+ **1** clove garlic, minced

+ **⅓ cup** sugar

+ **¼ teaspoon** MSG (see note)

+ **½ cup** peach nectar

+ **½ cup** soy sauce

In a large glass bowl, whisk together ginger, garlic, sugar, MSG, peach nectar, and soy sauce. Add the steaks or cubes and toss so that the meat is fully coated in the marinade. Cover with plastic wrap and refrigerate 8 hours or overnight, turning occasionally. Reserve the marinade.

The steaks can be prepared on a charcoal grill, broiled or pan-fried. Alternately, the cubes can be threaded onto skewers and grilled. Cook the meat, turning occasionally until the preferred doneness is achieved. Remove the steaks and transfer to a cutting board. Cover with foil and let rest for 5-10 minutes. Meanwhile, transfer the reserved marinade to a small saucepan. Bring to a gentle boil; cook until liquid is somewhat reduced. Slice the steak against the grain into thin strips. Serve the warmed sauce over the steak.

Note: You can leave out the MSG as I did or substitute sea salt.

Adapted from: Dining In - Baltimore by Bonnie Rapoport

Cherries Jubilee

Flaming dishes were all the rage at American fine dining establishments in the '60s and this is an old school classic with timeless appeal. It would be a fun and entertaining dessert choice to share with great friends.

Serves: 6

+ **1 can** dark, pitted Bing cherries, drained with juice reserved

+ **¼ cup** brandy

+ Sugar to taste (optional)

+ Vanilla ice cream

Heat a large skillet over an open flame. Add cherries, brandy and, if using, sugar. Once the cherries begin to release their juices take a large spoonful of the liquid and hold it next to the flame until it ignites. Return it carefully back to the skillet where the rest of the liquid should also ignite.

Turn off the heat and let the flames subside. If using an electric burner, ignite cherries right in the skillet and let the flames die out.

Pour some of the reserved juice over good vanilla ice cream. Top with cherries.

Adapted from: Dining In - Baltimore by Bonnie Rapoport

Tuscany - Canterbury

Jeannier's
105 West 39th Street

1988-2005

A culinary institution, Jeannier's was situated in the historic Tuscany-Canterbury neighborhood near Johns Hopkins University in Baltimore. Back in the day, many of the city's grandest apartment buildings were built to accommodate dining rooms, sparing residents the need to cook. Jeannier's was tucked away inside the Broadview apartments.

Roland Jeannier arrived in the States from the south of France in 1958 with the intention of cooking gourmet food. After originally settling in Boston, he was enticed to take on a chef's position in 1961 at Les Tuileries Restaurant in the Stafford Hotel in Mount Vernon. He worried that Baltimore might not be sophisticated enough for his cooking and planned to return to Boston. However, his wife Colette, became enamored with Baltimore, so with determination he set out to slowly introduce new gourmet food to a city that needed it.

Jeannier's served authentic, classic French food. Baltimore Sun food critic, John Dorsey, said that the restaurant "always had good food and was comfortable, it never was trendy or pretentious - it echoed Baltimore's character." Jeannier learned how to cook the local dishes and enjoyed fusing them into what he called "the best of France and Maryland."

Croque Madame a la Jeannier

Jeannier's delicious Croque Madame is a cross between French toast and a grilled ham and cheese sandwich. Any premium ham will work with the exception being Smithfield.

Serves: 1

+ **2** slices of bread
+ **4** thin slices of Swiss cheese
+ **4** thin slices of gourmet ham

+ **1** egg, beaten
+ **½ cup** milk

Beat together the egg and milk in a stainless-steel bowl with a whisk. Make your sandwich, placing the cheese on top of a bread slice and layering the ham and more cheese. Top with the second slice of bread. Grease a skillet with butter over moderate heat. Soak both sides of the sandwich in the egg mixture and sauté both sides until golden brown, about 2 minutes per side. Keep a watchful eye so it doesn't burn, but long enough to melt all the cheese through.

Adapted from: The Baltimore Sun, May 30, 1990

Jeannier's Spinach Fettucine with Smoked Salmon, Scallions and Goat Cheese

Anything but typical, this pasta dish is both quick and elegant.

Serves: 2

+ **6 to 8 ounces** spinach fettucine
+ **4 ounces** smoked salmon, cut into thin strips
+ **4 ounces** goat cheese log, cut into rounds
+ **2 tablespoons** fresh basil, julienned
+ **1** clove garlic, minced
+ **4** scallions, cut into 1" lengths
+ **4 tablespoons** butter
+ **1 tablespoons** olive oil
+ **1 tablespoon** white wine

Bring a large pot of water to a boil. Add pasta when boiling. Stir occasionally to keep from sticking. Melt butter in a sauté pan, add olive oil, garlic and scallions. Sauté over medium heat for 5 minutes. Add smoked salmon, fresh basil, and white wine and continue cooking over low heat.

When pasta is cooked, drain and briefly rinse with cold water (to keep it from cooking further). Toss in the sauté pan with the above ingredients. Serve on warmed plates.

Garnish with rounds of goat cheese and serve.

Adapted from: www.baltimoremd.com submitted by Cathy Adams

Mousseline Sauce

This sauce is delicious served with chilled seafood such as poached salmon, shrimp or jumbo lump crab cocktail.

Yield: 3 cups

+ **5 chef spoons** (see note) mayonnaise
+ **1 chef spoon** ketchup
+ **2 chef spoons** horseradish
+ **2 ounces** Jack Daniels or Gentleman Jack

+ **1 tablespoon** parsley, chopped
+ **2 tablespoon** Dijon mustard
+ Salt & white pepper to taste
+ **½ quart** heavy whipping cream

Mix together mayonnaise, ketchup, horseradish, Jack Daniels, parsley, Dijon mustard, and salt, and pepper. In a separate bowl, whip ½ quart heavy whipping cream to a peak. Fold the whipped cream gently into the mayonnaise mixture. Taste to see if there is enough horseradish; it should be a little pungent.

Note: A chef spoon is larger than an average spoon and holds an exact 2.5 tablespoons.

Adapted from: www.jackdaniels.co.za submitted by Mickey Graham, chef de cuisine at Jeannier's

Le Tullipe aux Framboise de Mason-Dixon Line

Pastry chef Jaye Ayres prepared this fresh raspberry dessert as part of a Maryland menu designed by chef Jeannier for the Baltimore international wine and food group, The Society of Bacchus. The meal was met with a standing ovation.

Serves: 6 to 8

+ Vanilla Ice Cream
+ Fresh raspberries and mint for garnish
+ Tullipes
+ **4 ounces** sweet butter
+ **½ cup** sugar
+ **¼ cup** egg whites
+ **6 ounces** flour
+ Almond essence to taste
+ Vanilla to taste

Preheat oven to 375°. Cream the butter and sugar; add flour. Whisk the egg white slightly and add to the mixture with the almond and vanilla. Mix well.

Cover a cookie sheet with parchment and by the large spoonful place the batter while spreading it with the back of the spoon until it reaches 6" in diameter. Repeat until the batter is used up. Bake until golden brown.

When they are cooked, working one at a time with a spatula, drape the cookie over a teacup while still soft pressing to form a tight cup. Allow to cool and turn right side up. You should now have a flat-bottomed cup with a curved rim at the top.

Raspberry Sauce:
+ **1 12-ounce** package frozen raspberries
+ **½ cup** sugar

In a saucepan heat raspberries and add sugar. Simmer until slightly thickened. Strain the seeds through a sieve.

Raspberry Mousse:
+ **½ pint** fresh whipping cream
+ **1 teaspoon** sugar
+ **½ package** unflavored gelatin
+ **2 egg whites**, beaten until stiff
+ Vanilla and almond extract to taste

Dissolve the gelatin in a small amount of hot water. Cool, but do not allow to set. Whip the cream together with sugar; add the cooled gelatin and continue to whip. Fold in beaten egg whites and a teaspoon of cooled raspberry sauce.

Gently place a small scoop of vanilla ice cream into the fragile tulip and then add a scoop of raspberry mousse. Drizzle sauce around the mousse and ice cream garnishing with fresh raspberries and mint sprigs.

Adapted from: The Evening Sun, July 16, 1986

Oysters Colette

Named for Mrs. Jeannier, this fresh oyster dish was a nod to the appreciation Baltimoreans hold for Maryland seafood.

Serves: 12

+ **2 dozen** oysters in the shell

+ **1-pound** butter, creamed

+ **2 ounces** anchovies

+ **2 ounces** white wine

+ **3 ounces** grated Parmesan cheese

+ **3 ounces** pimento

+ **2 tablespoons** parsley, chopped

+ **6 ounces** grated Swiss cheese

Preheat oven to 350°.

In a medium bowl, cream the butter. Blend in the anchovies, pimento, Parmesan cheese, and wine. Gently fold the chopped parsley into the mixture to avoid turning the mixture a green shade.

Shuck the oysters, leaving the oysters in the half shell. Take about a ½ teaspoon of the butter mixture and top each oyster, followed by a sprinkling of Swiss cheese. Place in oven, bake until the butter is melted, and serve.

Adapted from: The Baltimore Sun, January 31, 1982

Mount Washington

Café des Artistes
1501 Sulgrave Avenue

1978 - 1992

(O) pening a fine French restaurant in downtown Baltimore back in 1978 took a certain amount of courage and conviction. Baltimore was still undergoing a renaissance and Harborplace would not open for another two years. Steve Levinson met the challenge by opening the refined Café des Artistes. The restaurant's location next to the Mechanic Theater in Hopkins Plaza made it the ultimate venue for pre-and-post-theater dining and entertainment. What evolved was a celebrated reputation built upon its first-rate cuisine and lovely atmosphere.

The interior had a 1930s French elegance. Palettes of peach and beige enhanced the main dining room along with silver wine buckets and fresh roses. Adjacent to the dining room was the smaller and less formal Brasserie bar. The Brasserie, a piano bar, offered live entertainment nightly and a smaller menu, making it a perfect stop for an after-theater nightcap. When Oprah Winfrey left Baltimore for Chicago in 1983, WJZ threw her going away party at the Café. James Beard award-winning chef, Spike Gjerde, of Woodberry Kitchen, was once employed as a pastry chef there. Sometime during the mid-1980s Levinson chose to relocate Café des Artistes into its final home in the popular Mount Washington Village.

Foto-Thomson

Café des Artistes
Cuisine Française

VErnon 7-6600
9 Hopkins Plaza
Baltimore

Entertainment in
the Brasserie lounge from 9 P.M. until.

Special pre-theatre menu available.

Mussels Café des Artistes

Perfect for entertaining a large crowd.

Serves: 12

+ **2 quarts** mussels, rinsed, cleaned, and de-bearded
+ **1 tablespoon** onion, chopped
+ **1 cup** white wine
+ **1 tablespoon** shallots, finely chopped

+ **1-pint** heavy cream
+ **1 teaspoon** fresh dill
+ Salt and freshly ground pepper to taste
+ **2 pounds** angel hair pasta

Place mussels, shallots, onions, and white wine in a saucepan. Cover and cook slowly until mussels begin to open. Remove meat from shells, discarding any that do not open. Strain and reserve juices, adding cream and dill. Cook slowly until reduced by 1/3. Meanwhile, cook the pasta. Add mussels and pepper to sauce, cook until heated through, and serve over pasta.

Source: www.tapatalk.com, November 9, 2007

Loup en Croute a la Mousse Saint Jacques

Sea Bass in Pastry Crust with Sea Scallop Mousse

Serves: 6

+ **3 pounds** sea bass, cleaned and fileted

+ Fresh or dried fennel

+ Salt and white pepper to taste

+ Sea Scallop Mousse (recipe follows)

+ **2 pounds** puff pastry, homemade or commercial

+ **Egg wash:** 1 egg beaten with 1 teaspoon water

Preheat oven to 350°.

Sprinkle filets with fennel, salt, and white pepper. Set aside. Prepare the Sea Scallop Mousse. Using 1 pound of the puff pastry, roll out to a 20" by 12" oval to a thickness of ¼". The finished product should be fish-shaped. Place a 2" thick layer of mousse on the sheet of pastry allowing a margin of 3" all around. Place fish filets on top. Cover filets completely with the mousse. It is important that the mousse extend slightly beyond the edge of the filets.

Brush the exposed dough with the egg wash. Roll out another sheet of pastry and place it over the mousse. Press the edges onto the egg wash so the two pieces of dough stick together. Trim the edge of the pastry to resemble an oval fish shape. Use trimmed pastry to decorate the top like fish scales. Bake for 30 to 40 minutes.

Sea Scallop Mousse:
+ **1 ½ pounds** sea scallops

+ Salt

+ **2 tablespoons** chopped shallots

+ **1 tablespoon** brandy

+ **2 cups** heavy cream

+ **3** whole eggs plus **2** egg whites

+ **1 tablespoon** Pernod

+ Cayenne pepper

Puree the scallops, salt, shallots, and brandy in the container of a food processor or blender. Add the cream, whole eggs, and Pernod, blending again. Add the egg whites and again puree until the consistency is thick and mousse-like. Taste for seasoning. Add a pinch of cayenne pepper.

Adapted from: Dining In - Baltimore by Bonnie Rapoport

Fraises Romanoff

Romanoff's, a Beverly Hills restaurant owned by Michael Romanoff in the 40's and 50's, popularized the American version of this famous dessert. The original creation called Strawberries Americaine Style is credited to chef Escoffier from the Carlton Hotel in London but was later renamed Strawberries Romanoff at the namesake restaurant.

Serves: 6

+ **2 pints** strawberries
+ **¼ cup** Curaçao
+ **¼ cup** Cointreau
+ Dash of vinegar
+ **¼ to ½ cup** sugar
+ **2 cups** whipped cream

Wash and clean the berries. Macerate in the Curaçao, Cointreau, vinegar and sugar (to taste). Allow to sit for at least 3 hours. Spoon into a crystal serving bowl or individual bowls and top with whipped cream.

Adapted from: Dining In - Baltimore by Bonnie Rapoport

Parkville

Angelina's
7135 Harford Road
1952 - 2008

*E*veryone in Baltimore who loves crab cakes has a favorite establishment where they loyally return, but one simply can't deny that Angelina's was an all-time favorite for its signature dish. In 1952, Angelina "Miss Angie" Tadduni, her husband, Joe, and her sister and brother-in-law, Sarah and Sam Conigliaro opened this neighborhood Italian restaurant. The Conigliaros had been operating the corner rowhouse as a grocery store, but times were changing, and chain stores had begun to move into the neighborhood. So, the two couples joined forces and opened Angelina's. It sounded more Italian than Sarah's.

Miss Angie believed in quality over speed. Her father grew the tomatoes for her made-from-scratch spaghetti sauce and the neighborhood supported the business. Every day she would be in the kitchen by 7 AM with her pots of sauce simmering away.

Following Joe's death in 1968, the restaurant was sold to Bob and Carol Reilly. Bob was a trained chef. They asked Miss Angie to stay on in the kitchen, where she would continue to whip up her specialties until she retired in 1999 at the age of 84. In addition to keeping the Italian fare, the Reillys added an Irish pub downstairs naming it: O'Reilly's Shebeen. The pub was the first in Baltimore to serve Guinness Draught. Bob Reilly is generally credited with the creation of the Angelina's crab cake, which, with his own touches, became the signature dish of the restaurant. With name recognition came fame far beyond Parkville. Visitors and Baltimoreans alike savored Angelina's softball-sized crab cakes. In later years, Miss Angie said, "It's the same as everything. Top-quality food, top-quality ingredients, and you make everything from scratch." Angelina's was the recipient of over 30 awards for their Maryland crab cakes, in part by using only 100% Maryland blue crab (it's sweeter than its counterparts), 100% jumbo lump crabmeat, never pasteurized, and as little filler as possible.

The restaurant changed hands again in the '80s after Bob Reilly's passing. Now operated by Bob and Susan Bufano, once again Miss Angie was asked to remain at her post while Carol Reilly stayed on as General Manager. Even with their success, there was increasing demand for crab cakes from Baltimore and beyond. The Bufanos wisely recognized that an internet website would increase sales and further expand the business. While the restaurant eventually closed in 2008, the mail order business still operates as Angelina's of Maryland and ships throughout the U.S. Miss Angie passed away in 2008 at the age of 92, but Angelina's will forever remain synonymous with the mighty crab cake.

Angelina's Restaurant Crab Cakes

Whether or not this is the original "signature" recipe created by Bob Reilly is debatable, because according to lore the recipe went along with the sale of the restaurant. However, in a 1983 Baltimore Sun interview, Bob Reilly indicated that to every pound of crabmeat he would add "about 2 tablespoons of mayonnaise, an egg, a small amount of fresh breadcrumbs, white pepper and salt." So, this is probably not far off. In the summer I would often be recruited by my stepmother to make the 13-mile run over to Angelina's and pick up an order of the giant crab cakes for our family dinner. She never got an argument from me!

Yield: 10 crab cakes

+ **1-pound** lump crabmeat, picked
+ **1 cup** fresh bread crumbs
+ **1/3 cup** milk, approximately
+ **1** egg, lightly beaten
+ **¼ cup** mayonnaise
+ **½ teaspoon** baking powder
+ **2 teaspoons** onions, minced (optional)
+ **½ teaspoon** salt
+ **¼ teaspoon** ground white pepper
+ Flour for dusting
+ Butter or vegetable oil for frying

Place crab meat in a large bowl. Cover with bread crumbs and moisten with milk.

Combine beaten egg with the mayonnaise in a small bowl. Add baking powder, parsley, onion, salt, and pepper.

Pour over crab mixture and gently combine until well mixed. Form into 10 crab cakes. Place on plate and refrigerate for at least 1 hour.

Dust cakes lightly with flour. Heat butter or oil in pan until hot. Fry crab cakes until golden and drain on paper towels. Serve hot.

Adapted from: The Baltimore Sun, September 30, 2009

PART II: BALTIMORE COUNTY

Pikesville

The Pimlico
a.k.a. The Pimlico Hotel
1777 Reisterstown Road

1951 - 1991

*E*veryone gathered at the Pimlico on a Saturday night. It was a hub for activity
whether for dinner, celebrating, or talking politics. A part of the Pimlico's
attraction was that on Saturdays, and most other nights, it was like a Who's Who
of Baltimore. Located on Park Heights Avenue near the Pimlico Race Track, the
restaurant attracted not just horse racing fans, but also local politicians, sports
figures, celebrities and, of course, old friends.

Leon Shavitz and Nates Herr built the Pimlico Hotel restaurant on the success
of their Jewish deli, Nates and Leon's. In 1951 the partners bought the rundown
Pimlico Hotel (built in 1875) and turned the first floor into a restaurant. The friendly,
extroverted Shavitz greeted customers as if they were family. Everyone who went
there knew they could rely on great service and great food. Politicians often worked
the room when campaigning for office, and it was always a center for political
activity.

Monday Night Football sports luminaries, Howard Cosell, Frank Gifford, and Don
Meredith were known to drop in after a game. Other more local regulars included
Brooks Robinson, Jim Palmer, Johnny Unitas, and Oprah Winfrey before she became
a star. Oprah later recalled her first experience with a finger bowl was at the Pimlico
Hotel, "I was like, 'Okay, there's lemon in it.' I was two seconds away from drinking
it." When visiting Baltimore many internationally known performers came to the
restaurant. When the Rolling Stones performed at the Capital Centre in 1981 their
backstage spread, including a raw bar, was prepared by the Pimlico. It was a first-
class operation that at its peak offered a 14-page menu with more than 100 entrées.
Shavitz once even headed to a NYC Chinese employment agency in search of a chef,
so he could add authentic Chinese dishes to the menu. Some considered it to be the
best Chinese food in town.

In 1959, Shavitz suffered a heart attack and his two sons-in-laws, Lenny
Kaplan and Al Davis, joined the business. Thanks to their efforts, the Pimlico's
Cavalier Lounge also became a popular hangout featuring nightly entertainment.
Unfortunately, as the Park Heights neighborhood deteriorated many customers
began feeling uneasy about going there. By 1984 the Pimlico had relocated to the
county, moving into the Commerce Center on Reisterstown Road.

I must admit to a certain dismay at never having frequented the original Pimlico.
Regulars missed it too, insisting its new home just wasn't the same. The food and
service were still reliable, but the overall aura was lacking. I had lunch with my
grandmother on several occasions at the Commerce Center location, and I admit
I rather enjoyed the surroundings. The restaurant utilized colorful, contemporary
posters and large, comfortable red banquettes. From pickles to Coffey salads to
Chinese food; there was something for everyone at the Pimlico. The most famous

salad served at the Pimlico was the Coffey Salad, named for waitress Claudia Coffey, a thirty-year plus veteran. Miss Coffey developed the chopped salad, which came to be known as her signature. She constructed and tossed it tableside, always rubbing the wooden salad bowl with garlic and onion. Fans of the salad would try and duplicate it, but it was never quite the same. It wasn't that the ingredients were unusual, but it was the way she put them together that made it so good.

Coffey Salad

"So many people in town have tried to copy it, but they miss," said Al Davis. "It's usually too much vinegar." ~ The Baltimore Sun, February 27, 2002. This recipe approximates Miss Coffey's chopped salad

Serves: 1

+ ½ head iceberg lettuce, chopped

+ 1 slice onion, chopped

+ 2 slices tomato, chopped

+ ½ hard-boiled egg, chopped

+ 1 clove garlic, crushed

+ **1 teaspoon** oregano

+ **3 heaping teaspoons** grated Parmesan cheese

+ **2** chopped anchovies

+ Salad oil to taste

+ Vinegar to taste

Toss together the first 8 ingredients. Gradually mix in the oil and vinegar, adjusting to taste.

Adapted from: The Baltimore Sun, February 27, 2002

Pimlico Chopped Liver

Jerry Tucker first worked at Nates and Leon's deli before he was drafted to open the Pimlico Hotel. As word spread among diners, his recipe for chopped chicken liver became a house specialty. Gourmet Magazine requested it, but Tucker declined stating, "There are some secrets I'll keep."

+ **2 pounds** chicken livers
+ **1-pound** onions, chopped
+ **4** hard-boiled eggs

+ **1/3 cup** chicken fat
+ Salt and pepper to taste

In a skillet, sauté onions in chicken fat until well browned. Bring salted water to a boil and simmer chicken livers for 25 minutes. Strain. Place all ingredients in a food processor. Chill completely. Mound the chopped liver on a serving dish garnishing with additional hard-boiled eggs and Bermuda onions. Serve with crackers, French, or rye bread.

Adapted from: The Evening Sun, February 19, 1987

Veal Audrey

I prefer not to eat veal, but this recipe will also work very nicely with chicken breast scallopine.

Serves: 2

+ **12 to 14 ounces** prime veal, cut and pounded into small thin pieces **(1 ½ to 2 ounces each)**
+ Flour for dusting
+ **6 tablespoons** clarified butter
+ Salt and pepper to taste

+ **½ cup** dry white wine
+ **2 teaspoons** lemon juice
+ **1 teaspoon** shallots, chopped
+ **3 ounces** shelled, green pistachio nuts

Salt and pepper the veal; then lightly dust in flour. Brown lightly in butter on each side. Add white wine, lemon juice, shallots and pistachios. Simmer over medium heat until the sauce thickens slightly. Serve on a warmed platter.

Adapted from: Hunt to Harbor by The Junior League of Baltimore

Lady Baltimore Cake

Master pastry chef Jan Bandula often made this cake for guests when he worked at the Pimlico Hotel. This is a cooked icing, so you will need to have a candy thermometer on hand for this recipe.

Yield: 1 cake

For cake:
+ **8 ounces** butter, softened
+ **14 ounces** sugar
+ **¼ ounce** vanilla extract
+ **¼ ounce** almond extract
+ **13 ounces** cake flour

+ **1 tablespoon** baking powder
+ **¾ teaspoon** salt
+ **8 ounces** milk
+ **7 ounces** egg whites
+ **⅛ teaspoon** cream of tartar

Preheat oven to 375°.

Cream butter and sugar together until light and fluffy. Add the vanilla and almond extracts, mixing and scraping down the sides of bowl. Sift together dry ingredients. Alternate adding dry ingredients and milk to the butter/sugar mixture. Mix until smooth.

In a clean bowl, whip the egg whites and cream of tartar. Slowly, add sugar. Whip to soft peaks. Fold the whipped whites into the batter. Divide mixture evenly among three greased 9" cake pans. Bake for 35 minutes. Remove from oven and allow to cool on a wire rack.

For icing:
+ **1-pound** sugar
+ **6 ounces** water
+ Pinch of cream of tartar

+ **6 ounces** egg whites
+ **¼ ounces** vanilla extract

In a saucepan, combine sugar, water, and cream of tartar. Using a candy thermometer, cook the sugar to 265°.

In another bowl, whip egg whites at high speed to form medium peaks.

Very slowly, pour cooked sugar into whipped egg whites. Whip to slightly cool. Add vanilla.

For filling:
+ **3 ounces** pecans, lightly toasted

+ **5 ounces** dried fruit, chopped (raisins, figs, currants, candied cherries)

Combine and reserve for cake assembly.

Assembling Lady Baltimore cake:
Transfer one-third of the icing to a medium bowl. Stir fruit-and-nut filling into the icing.

Place one cake layer on a serving plate and add half the icing/filling mixture. Add a second cake layer on top. Spread second layer with remaining icing/filling. Place third layer on top. Frost the top and the sides of cake with plain icing.

Garnish with dried fruit and nuts.

Adapted from: www.chesapeaketaste.com

Pimlico Cake

This luscious Pimlico Cake recipe comes from chef Callie Tarts of The Classic Catering People. Gail Kaplan, a founding partner of Classic Catering, is the daughter of Leon Shavitz. Debby Lynch, a former pastry chef at the Pimlico, recalled that they used to sell 40 Pimlico cakes (each with 14 slices) per week.

Yield: 1 cake

+ 1 boxed cake mix of your choice (follow directions for one cake)
+ Favorite fudge frosting
+ Pastry Cream (recipe follows)

Pastry Cream:
+ **2 cups** whole milk
+ **¼ cup** sugar

+ **1 teaspoon** vanilla extract
+ Pinch of salt
+ **4 egg yolks**
+ **¼ cup** cornstarch
+ **¼ cup** sugar
+ **2 tablespoons** butter

Heat milk, ¼ cup sugar, vanilla and salt in a medium saucepan until it simmers. In a separate bowl, whisk together yolks, cornstarch, and remaining ¼ cup sugar. Pour hot milk mixture one cup at a time into yolk mixture. Pour this back into saucepan; cook over medium-high heat, whisking constantly until thick (about 2 minutes).

Transfer to a mixing bowl with a paddle. Add butter to hot mixture. Mix until cool (about 5 minutes).

Assembly:
Slice cake into 3 equal layers (set aside top 2 layers). Spread pastry cream onto cake layer, and top with cake layer (alternate until there are 2 layers of pastry cream and 3 layers of cake, ending with cake at top). Ice cake with favorite fudge frosting, chilling until ready to serve.

Adapted from: www.jmoreliving.com

Lutherville

Harvey's at Greenspring Station
2360 West Joppa Road

1979 - 2000

The always popular Harvey's - home of the power lunch set. Situated in the small but high-end shopping promenade of Greenspring Station, it was a local favorite. Baltimorean, Harvey Sugarman, was a trend setter for sure. Guests discovered a fun and novel menu composed of mostly salads, sandwiches, pastas and other house specialties. This extensive selection offered something for everyone, from vegan to gourmet and everything in between. Sugarman served a sumptuous Sunday buffet brunch before "brunch" was trendy, and he was one of the first in the area to introduce a calorie-conscious section on the menu called "Dieter's Dreams."

The busy establishment was generally noisy and packed, but diners could, in nice weather, opt for a table outside in the courtyard, where lights twinkled from the trees above. Entertainment was provided by musicians in the courtyard gazebo playing folk or classical music. Inside, the comfortable dining rooms displayed textured paint walls in atypical colors, and every table had a peppermill. Diners anticipated complimentary homemade cheese spread served with breadsticks.

Barbara's Boursin

Inspired by the complimentary cheese spread served at Harvey's, Barbara Rosenberg of Baltimore launched a search for the recipe. When she came up empty, she re-created it as Barbara's Boursin and contributed it to the Baltimore Sun. She thinks it is just as good as the one served at Harvey's and I agree. Thank you, Barbara!

Yield: About 1 cup

+ **8 ounces** cream cheese (regular or light, but not fat-free), slightly softened
+ **2 tablespoons** butter, at room temperature
+ **½ teaspoon** fresh lemon juice
+ **1** clove garlic, finely minced

+ **1 tablespoon** dried oregano
+ **⅛ teaspoon** cayenne pepper
+ **¼ teaspoon** salt
+ **2 tablespoons** fresh Italian parsley, very finely minced

Allow the cream cheese and butter to come to room temperature. Mix together all ingredients either by hand or with a mixer. Refrigerate at least 1 hour. Serve with crackers, breadsticks, or crudité. This keeps several days in the refrigerator or can be frozen.

Adapted from: The Baltimore Sun, March 18, 2014

2360 West Joppa Road
Lutherville, Maryland

harveys
Gourmet Kitchen

Catering

Private Banquet Rooms

Roast Turkey Breast with Apple Walnut Stuffing

This stuffed turkey roulade along with Honeyed Sweet Potatoes were included as "Dieter's Dreams" holiday offerings at Harvey's.

Serves: 16 (6-ounce portions)

+ **1 4 to 5-pound** boneless, skinless turkey breast
+ **½ loaf** whole-wheat bread, cubed
+ **1** egg white
+ **¼ cup** skim milk

+ **2** Granny Smith apples, skinned and diced
+ **¼ cup** chopped walnuts
+ **¼ cup** honey
+ Pepper to taste

Preheat oven to 350°.

Butterfly turkey breast (or have the butcher do it). In a medium bowl, combine bread, apples, egg white, skim milk, walnuts, and honey, mixing well. Spread stuffing evenly on butterflied breast. Fold breast over the stuffing forming a roll and secure with butcher's twine. Season the breast with pepper and place in an oven-roasting bag. Bake for 2 ½ hours.

Adapted from: The Baltimore Sun, November 18, 1992

Honeyed Sweet Potatoes

Serves: 16

+ **5 pounds** sweet potatoes, peeled
+ **1 cup** honey

+ Salt and pepper, to taste

Preheat oven to 350°.

Boil sweet potatoes until tender. Transfer to a roasting pan and drizzle with the honey. Add salt and pepper and bake until golden brown, about 15 minutes.

Adapted from: The Baltimore Sun, November 18, 1992

Rodgers Forge

The Golden Arm Restaurant
6354 York Road

1968 - 1994

*B*altimore Colts icons Johnny Unitas and Bobby Boyd opened the Golden Arm Restaurant in 1968. It was a neighborhood restaurant and piano bar in a shopping center on York Road in Towson. Unitas and Boyd were often on hand as their kitchen served up good steaks and seafood; nothing too inventive, and that was just fine with its clientele. The large dining room, trimmed in dark wood, had a cozy fireplace and was separated from the bar area by some sort of latticework wall. On the occasions I was there for lunch, the dining room was packed with a mostly mature crowd. The bar, a favorite among regulars, was 40 feet long and a painted mural hung behind it depicting the sudden-death victory of the Colts over the Giants in what is referred to as "The Greatest Game Ever Played." Many longtime Colt fans held grudges (many still do) against Robert Irsay, for packing up the team and relocating the franchise in a 1984 surprise overnight move. After that the men's room door was posted with a metal nameplate calling it the "Bob Irsay Room."

The bar crowd, whose taste tended to be a throwback to another era, enjoyed their Scotches and Manhattans, along with entertainment on the keyboards provided by Brad Wines and his bubble-making machine, reminiscent of Lawrence Welk. Regulars made the Golden Arm a hangout both before and after the game. Fans came for Sunday brunch before boarding chartered buses for Memorial Stadium. When they returned, players and coaches often followed for a post-game repast.

I thank my best friend, Meg, who grew up in nearby Stoneleigh, for my introduction to the Golden Arm. Meg was and is the "tuna fish sandwich connoisseur." I still affectionately tease her about giving her this title, because I knew she would invariably order the tuna sandwich, and I'm pretty sure the Golden Arm offered her favorite back in the day!

Baked Stuffed Mushrooms

A Maryland favorite, these crab imperial stuffed mushrooms are simply mouthwatering and would make a great holiday appetizer. They can be assembled ahead of time and popped into the oven just before guests arrive.

Yield: 24

+ **1-pound** Maryland backfin crabmeat
+ **1/3 cup** mayonnaise
+ **1** egg
+ **2 tablespoons** milk
+ **1 teaspoon** Worcestershire sauce
+ **1 teaspoon** dry mustard
+ **½ teaspoon** celery salt
+ **¼ teaspoon** pepper
+ **⅛ teaspoon** paprika
+ Pinch ginger
+ **2 tablespoons** cracker meal
+ **24** fresh mushrooms (about 2" to 3" in diameter)

For topping:
+ **1 cup** mayonnaise
+ **1** egg
+ **⅛ teaspoon** seafood seasoning
+ **2** dashes hot sauce

Preheat oven to 375°.

Remove cartilage from crabmeat carefully, keeping lumps intact. Place crabmeat in a large bowl and set aside.

In a small bowl, combine mayonnaise, egg, milk, Worcestershire sauce, mustard, celery salt, pepper, paprika, and ginger. Pour sauce over crabmeat, mixing gently but thoroughly. Carefully mix in cracker meal.

Clean and remove stems from mushrooms. Place mushrooms on a baking sheet stem side up and fill each mushroom with about 2 tablespoons crab mixture. Bake for 10 to 12 minutes or until crabmeat mixture begins to brown.

Mix together 1 cup mayonnaise, egg, seafood seasoning, and hot sauce. Top each mushroom generously with sauce and sprinkle with paprika. Place in oven and bake until topping is golden brown, about 5 to 7 minutes.

Adapted from: Maryland Seafood Cookbook II by Maryland Department of Agriculture.

Shrimp Salad

The #1 selling dish at the Golden Arm was their shrimp salad according to former manager Jim Considine. Recipes from the kitchen were never written down, but rather, cooked and prepared by taste and memory. Jim had a recent conversation with Idella Boone, who ran the kitchen and is fondly referred to as "Miss Del". She shared with him three factors that really added to the product: 1) The shrimp were always steamed the night before; 2) DO NOT OVERSEASON WITH OLD BAY - the dressing should take on a creamy hue; if it turns reddish-brown, you've added too much; and, 3) They used only the very best institutional grade of mayonnaise called Mrs. Filbert's Extra Heavy- Duty Mayonnaise. The measurements I adapted here worked out beautifully and will generously serve two.

Yield: 3 cups

+ **1-pound** steamed shrimp (21/25 count), peeled and deveined
+ **1-2** stalks celery, diced
+ **½ cup** mayonnaise (see note)
+ **1 teaspoon** freshly squeezed lemon juice
+ **¼ teaspoon** white pepper
+ **½ teaspoon** Old Bay seasoning
+ **½ teaspoon** Sexton* granulated chicken bouillon base (see note)

Dice shrimp into 1/2" pieces. Set aside. In a medium bowl, mix together mayonnaise, celery, lemon juice, white pepper, Old Bay and chicken base. Add the shrimp tossing to coat with the dressing and refrigerate until ready to serve.

Note: I suggest using your favorite brand of mayonnaise or you could make your own by adding additional eggs resulting in a richer texture.

* Jim indicated using a high-quality chicken base (such as Knorr's) with more chicken flavor than salt.

Source: As shared with me by Jim Considine, former manager of the Golden Arm Restaurant

Towson

Valley View Room at Hutzler's a.k.a. the Tea Room
1 Joppa Road & Dulaney Valley Road

1952 - 1990

I miss Hutzler's! If you grew up in Baltimore, you shopped at Hutzler's. Period. I don't think I fully appreciated just how special the store was until it was gone. Their Towson building, described as Art Deco, was a beautifully laid out department store where shoppers received personalized service and carefully curated merchandise. Just a stone's throw from Lutherville, the Towson store was Hutzler's first expansion into the county and the timing was perfect. Opening in 1952, the store quickly became a shopping and dining mecca for all of Baltimore.

My grandmother often took me shopping for clothes or shoes at Hutzler's. My grandfather sometimes accompanied her on these outings as well. I believe he particularly liked going to Hutzler's because he enjoyed having lunch in the Tea Room. My mother took me to Hutzler's too. When I turned fourteen she allowed me to get my ears pierced at the store. She had insisted that I wait so that I could look back on the event as a sort of rite of passage. It turns out, she was right. As I recall, we left the jewelry counter with my new ear studs intact and headed up to the Tea Room on the 3rd floor.

The Tea Room—officially the Valley View Room—was pretty and spacious, with walls covered in pastel-colored murals depicting fox hunting, the Baltimore Oriole, black-eyed Susan, and the Hampton Mansion. The wide expanse of floor-to-ceiling windows gave patrons a panoramic view of the Goucher College campus, Hampton Mansion, and Loch Raven beyond.

The food was simple and delicious, because the ingredients were the best. The Tea Room had its own bakery producing tasty cakes and cookies, in addition to their famous cheese bread. The cheese bread was sliced, toasted and used for tuna, shrimp, and chicken salad sandwiches. As teenagers, Meg and I would occasionally head to the Valley View Room for lunch, and—you probably guessed it—tuna salad on cheese toast.

Hutzler's Cheese Bread

Toasted slices of this homemade cheese bread make for the ultimate sandwich.

Yield: 4 loaves

+ **1 package (2 ¼ teaspoons)** active dry yeast
+ **1 cup** lukewarm water
+ **9 ½ cups** bread flour
+ **2 teaspoons** salt
+ **¼ cup** sugar
+ **2 cups** milk
+ **13 ½ ounces** sharp Cheddar cheese, grated **(about 3 ½ cups)**
+ **2 ¼ tablespoons** each margarine and butter

Preheat oven to 300°.

In a large bowl, dissolve the yeast in the water. Stir in the remaining ingredients. Knead the dough about 5 minutes and place it back in the bowl. Cover with a tea towel and allow it to rise until doubled, about 2 hours.

Divide the dough into 4 even parts and put it in greased 4"x 8" loaf pans. Let the loaves rise again and bake 1 hour.

Adapted from: www.thebakingsheet.com as submitted by John B. DeHoff of Cockeysville, September/October, 1995

Hutzler's Shrimp Salad

My boyfriend Mac loves his shrimp salad so when I found this recipe from Hutzler's I was anxious to try it out. The combination of medium and large shrimp pieces creates just the right texture for me. Add some toasted cheese bread for the "real" deal.

+ **2 cups** large cooked shrimp, peeled and deveined, cut into pieces
+ **2 cups** medium cooked shrimp, peeled and deveined, cut into pieces
+ **1 cup** celery, diced
+ **1 teaspoon** salt
+ **¼ teaspoon** pepper
+ **¼ teaspoon** Tabasco sauce
+ **1 teaspoon** Worcestershire sauce
+ **3 tablespoons** ketchup
+ **1 tablespoon** prepared mustard
+ **4 tablespoons** mayonnaise

Yield: 1 quart

Wring shrimp in paper towels until dry. Mix together the remaining ingredients. Stir in the shrimp and refrigerate. Serve on toasted cheese bread or on a bed of lettuce.

Adapted from: Baltimore's Bygone Department Stores: Many Happy Returns by Michael J. Lisicky

Hutzler's Potato Chip Cookies

A former Hutzler's employee shared this recipe with the Baltimore Sun indicating that she had found it in one of her old monthly employee newsletters. I wonder if they used Utz Originals?

Yield: 2 to 3 dozen cookies

+ **1-cup** butter, softened
+ **½ cup** sugar
+ **1 ½ cups** flour
+ **¼ teaspoon** salt
+ **½ cup** potato chips, crushed

+ **½ cup** chopped nuts
+ **1 teaspoon** vanilla
+ **1** egg yolk
+ Confectioner's sugar, if desired

Preheat oven to 350°.

With a hand mixer, cream together butter and sugar until smooth. Add egg yolk and vanilla mixing until fully incorporated. Mix in flour, salt, and nuts. Fold in potato chips. Drop cookie dough by tablespoonful onto ungreased baking sheets and bake on center rack for about 20 minutes or until edges are golden brown. Cool completely on a wire rack and dust liberally with powdered sugar.

Adapted from: The Baltimore Sun, October 7, 2014

Goucher Cake

This classic yellow cake is a Hutzler's original named for the nearby college. I just call it a mouth party!

Yield: 1 cake, serving 8 to 10

+ **1 cup** butter or margarine
+ **1 ¾ cups** sugar
+ **3 ¼ cups** cake flour
+ **5 teaspoons** baking powder
+ **¾ teaspoons** salt
+ **1 cup** milk
+ **1 teaspoon** almond extract
+ **4 egg** whites
+ Chocolate Icing (recipe follows)
+ Buttercream Icing (recipe follows)
+ **¼ cups** chopped almonds, toasted, for garnish

Preheat oven to 350°. In a large bowl, cream together butter and sugar. Sift dry ingredients together adding them alternately with the milk and almond extract. Mix thoroughly. With a hand mixer, beat egg whites until stiff and fold into batter. Pour batter into 2 greased and floured 9" cake pans. Bake 35 minutes or until a toothpick comes out clean.

Cool completely before spreading the chocolate icing between layers and on the sides of the cake. Spread the buttercream icing on the top. Sprinkle with toasted almonds.

Chocolate Icing:
+ **2 ounces** good bitter chocolate
+ **⅓ cup** butter
+ **½ cup** sugar
+ **½ cup** water
+ **¾ cup** powdered sugar
+ **3 egg** yolks
+ **¼ teaspoon** vanilla extract

Over low heat, melt chocolate and butter. Add both sugars and water. Cook until fully incorporated. Add the egg yolks and vanilla extract and cook 5 minutes. Ice between layers and along sides of cake.

Buttercream Icing:
+ **2 cups** powdered sugar
+ **2 tablespoons** butter, softened
+ **½ teaspoon** vanilla extract

Cream ingredients together and spread on top of cake.

Adapted from: The Baltimore Sun, December 21, 2006

Timonium

Shane's
1924 York Road

1977 - 1989

*I*n 1983, former Baltimore Sun restaurant critic, Elizabeth Large, wrote, "You don't know eclectic until you've seen Shane's dining rooms." When Peter Angelos bought the former Tail of the Fox, a private dining club, in the late '70s, he renamed it Shane's. It garnered attention with reports that $3 million had gone into the sumptuous décor. It was described as "preposterously grand." Adorned with stained glass window panels, brass railings and crystal chandeliers, some thought it was over-the-top opulent. The Custer Room's siding came from General George Custer's parents' homestead, while its grand rosewood fireplace was thought to have come from the Singer mansion. The staircase and upstairs bar had originally graced a luxury passenger steamer of yore, the City of Detroit III. It became what may have been the most popular dinner spot in the county. I opted to hold my wedding rehearsal dinner at Shane's back in 1988 after enjoying many previous dinners there.

Angelos recruited executive chef, Wilfred Paul Crowninshield, to Baltimore from Philadelphia to open Shane's. He became famous for his recipe for frosted crab soup, his own creation, which rounded out the Continental menu.

The lower space was utilized primarily for live entertainment and dancing with the house band, Shane's Fancy. Many will remember taking in stage productions of "Gypsy" or "Fiddler on the Roof" at Shane's. These were just two of the shows performed there by the Baltimore Actors' Theatre.

Frosted Crab Soup

This original recipe was created and brought to Baltimore by "Chef Paul" Crowninshield. I understand that it's still a much-in-demand menu staple at the Maryland Club, where he was executive chef from 1979 to 1989.

Serves: 8 to 10

+ **5 cans** of tomato soup **(50 ounces)**
+ **46 ounces** bottle tomato juice
+ **3 pints** sour cream
+ **3 tablespoons** Old Bay seasoning
+ **3 tablespoons** fresh lemon juice
+ **3 tablespoons** Worcestershire sauce
+ Salt and white pepper, to taste
+ **1-pint** jumbo lump crabmeat

Blend together first 7 ingredients. Adjust seasonings to taste. Add pint of crabmeat. Chill completely before serving.

Adapted from: www.tastebook.com

Sportmen prefer their
Luncheons, Dinners
and Cocktails at

PEERCE'S

**DULANEY
VALLEY ROAD
PHOENIX, MD.**

County Atmosphere

Five Fireplaces

For Reservations

Phone CL 2-3100

"*Just* 10 Minutes drive from *Towson* on Dulaney Valley Rd."

Phoenix

Peerce's Plantation
12460 Dulaney Valley Road

1937-2001

"Stay on this side of the bridge, mind your own business and kill them with politeness," Duff Lake cautioned his son, Peerce, offering this final advice as he handed over the keys to the family business. It was 1963 and Peerce's Plantation was located just northeast of the bridge that stretched across Loch Raven Reservoir in Baltimore County. The restaurant overlooked pastoral views of the pine trees and the tranquil waters of the reservoir.

William Peerce, Peerce Lake's uncle, had opened Peerce's Corner in 1937. It was a convenience store for farmers providing dry goods, beer, soda, and gas pumps. Lake's mother, Marie, began selling her fried chicken at a farm equipment expo that had been held on the property in 1941. In reaction to requests and encouragement from farm visitors who enjoyed Marie's fried chicken, crab cakes, and country ham feasts, Peerce's Corner emerged as a restaurant. Initially, the new establishment offered only outdoor patio dining, but as its popularity grew an inside dining room was added, and the name was changed to Peerce's Plantation.

After Peerce took over the business, he transformed it into a more upscale restaurant. By 1975, Peerce's was under the stewardship of Manager Rudi Paul (who would later open Rudi's 2900 Restaurant) and his friend, Executive Chef Josef Gohring (later of Josef's Country Inn). Peerce's specialized in Continental cuisine and Maryland seafood favorites. Waiters presented fresh entrée cuts on a display tray, assisting diners in narrowing their selections. Just thinking about that tray of choices reminds me of my mother, who, if it was in season, always selected the Shad Roe. Though it wasn't the most enticing item to me, that's where I got a quick education on fish eggs.

With its crackling fireplace the Lake Room was warm and inviting, while the Plantation Room and porch were resplendent with white-painted wrought iron accents which served as the architectural hallmark of Peerce's. My family and I spent more than one Christmas Eve dinner at Peerce's and it felt like home away from home. We were together to share the spirit of Christmas and enjoy a fine dinner in front of the warm fire burning in the stone fireplace. The restaurant was always a premier gathering spot whether the occasion was a birthday, wedding, anniversary, bar mitzvah, prom night, or graduation. During its heyday in the '80s, Peerce's would serve more than 400 dinners on a Saturday night. A high school boyfriend of mine had an older brother who was a waiter at Peerce's. I was always thrilled when we were seated in his section, because he went the extra mile to offer my family an exceptional experience. The setting was just so welcoming, not only because of the beautiful drive out through Loch Raven, but once you arrived you knew there was a wonderful meal in store.

Peerce Lake should have taken his father's advice. Instead he opened a second location, Peerce's Downtown in 1980. Due to growing competition he was forced to close that one in 1988. By now people were becoming more health conscious and sought out lighter fare instead of rich Continental food. Peerce's downfall may have been its inability or desire to keep up with the trends. By 2001, as losses mounted, Lake was forced to close its doors.

Clams Casino

I tried my first order of Clams Casino at Peerce's and fell hard. This recipe will always be a classic in my book, although today I might eliminate the addition of MSG.

Makes: 24

+ **24** Cherrystone clams in shell
+ **6** slices bacon
+ **1** medium onion, minced
+ **½** green pepper, minced
+ **2 tablespoons** chives, chopped
+ **2 tablespoons** grated parmesan cheese
+ **1 teaspoon** paprika
+ **¼ teaspoon** ground white pepper
+ **2 to 3 dashes** seafood seasoning
+ Dash MSG

Preheat oven to 400°.

Open shells, letting each clam remain in one half. In medium skillet sauté bacon until crisp reserving the fat. Crumble the bacon and set aside. Pour off the excess fat in the skillet, adding onion and pepper and sauté for another 5 minutes.

In small bowl, mix together chives, cheese, paprika, pepper, seafood seasoning, and MSG. Blend into sautéed vegetables and then add the crumbled bacon.

Place 1 teaspoon of bacon mixture on each opened clam. Place clams on shallow baking sheet and bake for 10 minutes. Serve with melted or drawn butter.

Drawn Butter:
+ **2 tablespoons** butter
+ **2 tablespoons** flour
+ **½ teaspoon** salt
+ **⅛ teaspoon** pepper
+ **1 cup** hot water
+ **1 teaspoon** lemon juice
+ **2 tablespoons** butter

In a saucepan melt 2 tablespoons butter. Slowly add flour, salt, and pepper, stirring until smooth. Slowly stir in water and simmer 5 minutes. Remove from heat and add lemon juice. Stir in the butter, a little at a time.

Makes 1 cup.

Adapted from: Maryland Seafood Cookbook II by the Maryland Department of Agriculture

Oysters Buccaneer

The prized oyster juice should never be discarded because it adds amazing briny flavor and that is why its referred to as the liquor.

Serves: 6

+ **1-pound** Maryland backfin crabmeat

+ **3 tablespoons** butter or margarine

+ **½ teaspoon** salt

+ **⅛ teaspoon** pepper

+ Dash MSG

+ **1-pint** shucked Maryland oysters, with liquor

+ **1 tablespoon** butter or margarine

+ **1/8 teaspoon** seafood seasoning

+ **6** slices toast

+ **3 ounces** Smithfield ham, thinly sliced

+ Parsley, for garnish

+ Drawn or melted butter, if desired (see previous page)

Clean cartilage from crabmeat. In medium skillet, sauté crabmeat in 3 tablespoons butter for 3 minutes. Blend in salt, pepper and MSG and set aside.

In a saucepan, sauté oysters with their liquor in 1 tablespoon butter just until edges curl. Add seafood seasoning.

Place toast slices on a serving platter (or 6 individual plates). Add crabmeat, evenly distributing it over toast. Put 4 to 5 oysters on each portion and spoon desired amount of oyster liquid over oysters. Place ham slices on top. Garnish with parsley and serve with drawn butter, if desired.

Adapted from: Maryland Seafood Cookbook II by the Maryland Department of Agriculture

A family dinner enjoyed on the patio of Peerce's.

Shrimp Operngalleren

Chef Josef Gohring's signature recipe for Shrimp in Dill Sauce.

Serves: 4

+ **24** medium-sized shrimp, peeled and deveined
+ **2 tablespoons** oil
+ Salt and pepper to taste
+ **1 ½ teaspoons** fresh dill, chopped or ½ teaspoon dried dill
+ **¾ cup** Fish Velouté (recipe follows)
+ Lemon juice to taste
+ **1 to 2 tablespoons** Hollandaise sauce (see index)

Sauté the shrimp in oil until just cooked, about a minute. Add salt and pepper. Mix in dill and fish velouté. Stir in lemon juice and just before serving, mix in the Hollandaise sauce. Remove from heat.

Fish Velouté:
+ 1 celery stalk, finely chopped
+ 1 carrot, finely chopped
+ 1 onion, finely chopped
+ 1 cleaned leak, finely chopped
+ **3 tablespoons** butter
+ 1 bay leaf
+ 1 whole clove
+ **1-pound** Dover sole or grouper fish bones washed
+ **1 tablespoon** butter
+ **1 tablespoon** flour

Gently cook the mirepoix (chopped vegetables) in 3 tablespoons butter until they start to become tender. Do not brown. Add the bay leaf, clove, and fish bones. Cover completely with cold water, bring to a boil and reduce the heat to a very gentle simmer. Simmer for 2 hours and strain.

Make a roux by melting the remaining 1 tablespoon butter and blending in the flour. Cook for 2 to 3 minutes over moderate heat. Whisk in about ¾ cup of fish stock and bring the sauce to a gentle simmer. Season with salt and pepper.

Adapted from: Beyond Beer and Crabs by Maryland Chapter Arthritis Foundation

Lobster Thermidor

A French dish, the original recipe for Lobster Thermidor was created by Auguste Escoffier around 1880. This recipe might be just the ticket when planning a retro dinner party that will "wow" your guests.

Serves: 6

+ ¼ **cup** butter or margarine
+ 1 **4-ounce** can sliced mushrooms
+ ½ **cup** diced green bell pepper
+ ¼ **cup** flour
+ 1 **teaspoon** salt
+ ½ **teaspoon** dry mustard

+ Dash cayenne pepper
+ 2 **cups** milk
+ ¾ **pound** cooked lobster meat, cut in 1/2" **cubes (2 ½ cups)**
+ Grated parmesan cheese, for sprinkling
+ Paprika, for sprinkling

Preheat oven to 400°.

In a large saucepan, melt butter and sauté the mushrooms and green peppers for 5 minutes. In a small bowl mix flour, salt, dry mustard, and cayenne pepper together. Stir into the vegetable mixture, add milk gradually, and stir constantly until mixture thickens. Stir in lobster meat.

Spoon mixture into six well-greased lobster shells or individual casseroles. Sprinkle with Parmesan and paprika. Bake for 10 minutes or until cheese browns.

Adapted from: Maryland Seafood Cookbook by the Maryland Department of Agriculture

Recipe Index

Sauerbraten, *Haussner's*, 18

Smithfield Ham and Crab Sauté, *Haussner's*, 19

Steak Diane, *Danny's*, 56

Teriyaki Steak Chesapeake, *Chesapeake Restaurant*, 63

Veal Audrey, *Pimlico Restaurant*, 81

Meatless:

Eggplant Manicotti, B*rass Elephant Restaurant*, 41

Poultry:

Chicken Chestertown, *Louie's Bookstore and Café*, 46

Chicken Salad, *Women's Industrial Exchange*, 34

Paella Parellada, *Brass Elephant Restaurant*, 42

Roast Turkey Breast with Apple Walnut Stuffing, *Harvey's*, 87

Saltimbocca alla Romana, *Velleggia's*, 23

Seafood:

Angelina's Crab Cakes, *Angelina's*, 76

Baked Shad Stuffed with Roe, *Danny's*, 53

Baked Stuffed Shrimp, *Obrycki's*, 10

Chesapeake Bay Crabs, *Obrycki's*, 9

Crabe en Chemise (Crab Crepes), *Danny's*, 54-55

Crab Imperial, *Chesapeake Restaurant*, 62

Crab Imperial, *John Eager Howard Room*, 50

Haussner's Crab Imperial, *Haussner's*, 20

Jeannier's Spinach Fettucine with Smoked Salmon, Scallions and Goat Cheese, 67

Lobster Cardinale, *Marconi's*, 31

Lobster Thermidor, *Peerce's Plantation*, 103

Loupe en Croute a la Mousse Saint Jacques (Sea Bass in Pastry Crust with Sea Scallop Mousse), *Café des Artistes*, 73

Macheroni alla Pescatore (Seafood Pasta), *Velleggia's*, 24

Maryland Crab Cakes, *Obrycki's*, 11

Mussels Café des Artistes, *Café des Artistes*, 72

Paella Parellada, *Brass Elephant Restaurant*, 42

Rockfish in a Potato Crust with a Plum Tomato Compote and Brown Butter-Balsamic Vinaigrette, 5

Shrimp Charles, *Haussner's*, 19

Shrimp Operngalleren (Shrimp in Dill Sauce), *Peerce's Plantation*, 102

Shrimp Scampi, *Velleggia's*, 25

Sole Louis XV, *Danny's*, 57

SALADS

Chicken Salad, *Women's Industrial Exchange*, 34

Coffey Salad, *Pimlico Restaurant*, 80

German Potato Salad, *Haussner's*, 15

Italian Chopped Salad, *Marconi's*, 30

Obrycki's Coleslaw, *Obrycki's*, 10

Salade Beatrice, *Danny's*, 57

Shrimp Salad, *Golden Arm Restaurant*, 90

Hutzler's Shrimp Salad, *Valley View Room*, 93

Tomato Aspic, *Women's Industrial Exchange*, 34

Recipe Index

About the Author

Shelley Howell is a proud native Baltimorean with a passion for the past. A vintage enthusiast, her collection of recipes from now-defunct Baltimore restaurants is a treasure trove that will transport readers to another time and age. Shelley feels very fortunate to have personally dined at these sorely missed establishments and wants to resurrect them here to share with you. An animal lover, Shelley lives in Towson and volunteers with the Maryland SPCA. You can visit her Facebook page at Facebook.com/shelleyhowellauthor or email her at sahowell61@gmail.com to share restaurant memories or recipes.

.

Made in the
USA
Middletown, DE